AMISH
QUILTS

Edited by
Karen Bolesta

Rodale Press, Emmaus, Pennsylvania

Editor: *Karen Bolesta*
Technical Editor: *Karen Costello Soltys*
Technical Writer: *Janet Wickell*
Quilt Scout: *Bettina Havig*
Cover and Interior Designer: *Denise M. Shade*
Book Layout: *Nancy J. Smola*
Photographer: *Mitch Mandel*
Illustrators: *Mario Ferro and Jackie Walsh*
Copy Editor: *Erana Bumbardatore*
Manufacturing Coordinator: *Jodi Schaffer*
Editorial Assistance: *Stephanie Wenner*

Distributed in the book trade by St. Martin's Press

2 4 6 8 10 9 7 5 3 1 paperback

RODALE HOME AND GARDEN BOOKS

Vice President and Editorial Director: *Margaret J. Lydic*
Managing Editor, Quilt Books: *Suzanne Nelson*
Art Director: *Michael Mandarano*
Associate Art Director: *Mary Ellen Fanelli*
Studio Manager: *Leslie Keefe*
Copy Director: *Dolores Plikaitis*
Office Manager: *Karen Earl-Braymer*

We're happy to hear from you.
If you have any questions or comments concerning the editorial content of this book, please write to:
Rodale Press, Inc.
Book Readers' Service
33 East Minor Street
Emmaus, PA 18098
For more information about Rodale Press and the books and magazines we publish, visit our World Wide Web site at:
http://www.rodalepress.com

The quilt shown on pages 112–113 is owned by Doris Adomsky of Ivyland, Pennsylvania.

The photographs on pages 70, 86, and 96 appear courtesy of The Quilt Complex, San Anselmo, California.

Quote on page v reprinted with permission from *The Amish Quilt* by Eve Wheatcroft Granick, Good Books, Intercourse, Pennsylvania.

ISBN 0–87596–971–2 paperback
The Library of Congress has cataloged the hardcover edition as follows:
The classic American quilt collection. Amish / edited by Karen Bolesta.
   p. cm.
   ISBN 0–87596–725–6 (hardcover : alk. paper)
   1. Patchwork—United States—Patterns. 2. Quilting—United States—Patterns. 3. Quilts, Amish—United States. I. Bolesta, Karen
TT835.C575 1996
746.46—dc20   95–50617

Contents

ACKNOWLEDGMENTS

Amish Homage, made by Barbara Shiffler of Louisville, Kentucky. Barbara has been quilting for over ten years. Her quilt, named to honor early Amish quiltmakers, was exhibited at the Quilters' Heritage Celebration show in Lancaster, Pennsylvania, in April 1995.

81 Patch, owned by Shelly Zegart of Louisville, Kentucky. Shelly was a founding director of The Kentucky Quilt Project, the first state documentation project. She collects, writes, advises quilt survey groups, and sells fine quilts. She also lectures on all aspects of quilt history and aesthetics and has curated exhibitions here and abroad. Shelly is a founder and editor of *The Quilt Journal.*

Split Bars, made by Stan Book of Upland, California. Stan enjoys designing Amish-style quilts and designs as he pieces, working from the center of the quilt out to the borders. His fascination with color perception theory and the interaction of colors forms the foundation for his quilt designs. Stan's quilts have been featured in numerous exhibits and galleries, including two solo exhibits in California.

Double Irish Chain, owned by Bryce Hamilton of Minneapolis, Minnesota. A quilt dealer, Bryce specializes in contemporary Amish designs and has collected antique quilts for over 20 years. This quilt was made around 1930 in Holmes County, Ohio.

Broken Dishes, owned by Sandy Freeman of Allentown, Pennsylvania. Sandy is a freelance illustrator and frequently produces artwork for quilting books. She was shopping for a primitive yet contemporary quilt for her home when she came across Carole Dorr, a cottage-industry quilter who sells handmade quilts out of her farmhouse. Carole planned and pieced this quilt to Sandy's specifications, then passed it along to Helen Ellison, who added the hand-quilted accents.

Robbing Peter to Pay Paul, made by Becky Herdle of Rochester, New York. A quiltmaker and teacher, Becky enjoys making traditional quilts with a colorful twist. Her book, *Time-Span Quilts: New Quilts from Old Tops,* was released in 1994. She is a member of the Genesee Valley Quilt Club, which has existed for almost 60 years.

Chinese Coins Variation, made by Karan Flanscha of Cedar Falls, Iowa. Karan is a quiltmaker and teacher and has served as president of both the Iowa Quilters Guild and the Keepsake Quilters Guild. This quilt was shown in the Invitation Exhibit at the Kentucky Fall Festival of Quilts in 1989 and was featured in the June 1991 issue of *Quilter's Newsletter Magazine.*

Log Cabin, owned by Abner Schlabach of Perkasie, Pennsylvania. This quilt was repaired about ten years ago when the family discovered that moths had damaged it. Abner's mother, whose maiden name was Lulu Miller, led a family discussion on whether replacing a few strips would lessen the quilt's value, then decided to carefully proceed.

Double Nine Patch, owned by Douglas Tompkins of Puerto Montt, Chile. Douglas is a quilt collector and has focused his collecting on Amish quilts. Many of his quilts travel the country in an exhibition organized by Julie Silber of The Quilt Complex in San Anselmo, California. This quilt was loaned by The Quilt Complex.

Sparkle Plenty, made by Joan Dyer of Redondo Beach, California, and hand quilted by Mrs. Simon Ray Miller of Ohio. Joan presented this quilt to her daughter and son-in-law, Cheryl and Jesse Berg, of San Francisco, at their February 1994 wedding. Joan has been quilting since 1989. This quilt was included in the American Quilter's Society Tenth Annual Quilt Show in Paducah, Kentucky.

Sunshine and Shadow, owned by Douglas Tompkins of Puerto Montt, Chile. This Sunshine and Shadow quilt is typical of the 1940s time period for the Lancaster County Amish. The accepted color palette had expanded and the use of bright colors, many of them in a single design, was popularized. Julie Silber, of The Quilt Complex, was instrumental in allowing this quilt to be showcased.

Roman Stripe, owned by Susie Tompkins of San Francisco, California. This quilt is part of the Esprit Quilt Collection, an internationally renowned collection of Amish quilts that is exhibited in numerous museums and galleries; many of these museums have broken previous attendance records when the quilts were on display.

INTRODUCTION

Amish quilts reflect both the interaction with and the avoidance of "English" culture, which the group has practiced successfully for two and a half centuries. These quilts bridge two worlds, enriching our vision of the Amish community and illuminating the larger world of American quiltmaking and textile arts.
—Eve Wheatcroft Granick, *The Amish Quilt*

It's impossible to study the art of quiltmaking without recognizing the significant contribution that the Amish made to the patterns and colors we use so prevalently today. From the first glimpse of an authentic Amish quilt, it is apparent that the shapes and styles of the quilt closely reflect the culture and simplicity of Amish life. The symbolism of the pattern names themselves lends credence to the notion that religion, social conformity, and morality are foremost in the minds of Amish quiltmakers.

When the Amish immigrated to America in the eighteenth century, quiltmaking was not among the skills they brought with them. It is believed that their new neighbors passed along the basics, and the Amish ladies quickly adopted this new art.

Amish quilts are fascinating to us not only because they represent a unique style of quiltmaking but also because they represent a way of life we can only imagine. Amish quiltmakers have a knack for combining solid colors with familiar block patterns to create stunning quilts. And the simplicity of the designs makes it seem effortless. But those of us who have tried to execute a "simple" design realize what it takes to get from an idea to a finished quilt top. Wouldn't it be fun to sit in on a real "quilting," knowing that it takes a handful of nimble-fingered Amish ladies just a day and a half to quilt a bed-size quilt?

I am fortunate to have grown up just two hours from Lancaster County, Pennsylvania, one of the largest Amish communities in America. My family made countless trips to the Lancaster countryside each year to sample the homemade goodness we found there.

While commercialism and tourism have changed Amish quiltmaking forever, we can still celebrate the history behind the beloved quilt patterns we associate with the Amish. In this volume, we've gathered many of the most popular Amish designs and presented several antique quilts along with their contemporary counterparts. Since early examples of Amish quilts are rare, the vintage quilts included represent styles of the early twentieth century and two of the largest Amish counties—Lancaster, Pennsylvania, and Holmes, Ohio.

Most of the projects in this book are relatively easy to make, but some are more time consuming than others. We've assigned a skill rating to each quilt in relation to the others shown, so even a quilt that's rated as intermediate may be achievable by a confident beginner. And the intermediate or advanced quilter shouldn't shy away from an easy skill rating; the charm of an Amish quilt is as much in the selection of colors as in the actual task of piecing. We've even included an additional quilt size category to pay homage to the Amish style of quiltmaking. The new "bed topper" size takes advantage of the traditional square shape of many Amish designs; you can combine this comforter-size quilt with a dust ruffle to create an ensemble to fit today's standard bed sizes.

Unless you are Amish, you cannot make a true Amish quilt in literal terms. You can, however, make an Amish-style quilt that continues the tradition of combining simple shapes and breathtaking colors. As you work on your quilting project, take a few moments to read the history behind each quilt. Part of the romance of making an Amish-style quilt is the deep symbolism and humility that this quilt genre represents.

Karen Bolesta

Karen Bolesta

AMISH
PROJECTS

AMISH HOMAGE

Skill Level: *Easy*

*O*ne of the most recognized Amish patterns, this center diamond design represents tradition with a very noticeable twist. While the pattern is typically Amish, the color-splashed batik fabric and pieced corner blocks are definitely not! Quiltmaker Barbara Shiffler of Louisville, Kentucky, says she finds hand quilting to be the most enjoyable part of quiltmaking and says that as she quilted the last section, she quilted fewer and fewer hours each day just to make it last longer.

BEFORE YOU BEGIN

This quilt was inspired by the popular Diamond in the Square pattern and features basket blocks, rather than solid squares, at the corners of the quilt. The quilt's center features a square surrounded by two colors of triangles. It is easily assembled using quick-cutting and quick-piecing techniques. For information on rotary cutting, see page 115.

Three quilt sizes are included with these instructions. The layout and basic directions are the same for all three; only the dimensions of fabric pieces change from quilt to quilt. The bed topper category is a unique addition; since the quilt is square, it won't fit a double bed properly. It will, however, be ideal as a comforter when combined with a dust ruffle.

CHOOSING FABRICS

The vibrant batik fabric, used in the quilt's center and again in the baskets, is a departure from Amish tradition, but harmonizes with the quilt's red and purple fabrics to create an almost glowing effect.

This batik is mottled with warm pink and purple and cool blue and green. The bright red solid provides visual contrast with all the fabrics used, while the purple solid closely matches the batik's purple shadings. If a batik print is not for you, try a traditional

Quilt Sizes

	Wallhanging	Bed Topper (shown)	King
Finished Quilt Size	35½" × 35½"	70" × 70"	105½" × 105½"
Finished Block Size			
Basket	6"	12"	18"
Center Diamond	9½"	19"	28½"

Materials

	Wallhanging	Bed Topper	King
Black solid	¾ yard	2⅞ yards*	4¼ yards*
Red solid	¾ yard	2 yards	3⅝ yards*
Multicolor batik	¾ yard	1½ yards	1⅞ yards
Purple solid	⅜ yard	1⅛ yards	2 yards
Backing	1¼ yards	4¼ yards	9½ yards
Batting	42" × 42"	76" × 76"	112" × 112"
Binding	⅜ yard	⅝ yard	⅞ yard

NOTE: *Yardages are based on 44/45-inch-wide fabrics that are at least 42 inches wide after preshrinking.*

Borders are cut lengthwise to avoid seams; however, you will have leftover fabric. If you'd prefer to purchase less yardage, cut the borders on the crosswise grain and piece them. For the black solid, purchase 1⅞ yards for the bed topper and 3¾ yards for the king. For the red solid, purchase 3 yards for the king.

Cutting Chart

Fabric	Used For	Wallhanging		Bed Topper		King	
		Strip Width	Number of Strips	Strip Width	Number of Strips	Strip Width	Number of Strips
Black	Outer border	6½"	4	12½"	4*	18½"*	4
Red	Center triangles	7⅝"	1	14⅜"	1	21⅛"	2†
	Basket handles	12"	1	25"	1	22"	1
	Basket feet	1⅞"	1‡	2⅞"	1‡	3⅜"	1‡
	Basket	4⅞"	1‡	8⅞"	1	10⅞"	2‡
	Inner border	2½"	2	4½"	4	6½"	4
Batik	Center square	10"	1	19½"	1	29"	1
	Basket handles	12"	1	25"	1	22"	1
	Basket background	4⅞"	1‡	8⅞"	1‡	10⅞"	1
Purple	Center triangles	10⅜"	1	19⅞"	1	29⅜"	2
	Basket sides	1½"	2‡	2½"	2	3½"	8‡
	Inner border corners	2½"	1‡	4½"	1	6½"	4‡
	Basket bottom	2⅞"	1‡	4⅞"	1	5⅞"	1

* Cut lengthwise.

† If your fabric is 42½ inches wide or wider, cut only one strip. You will also need to cut one 3⅜-inch strip for the basket feet and one 10⅞-inch strip for the baskets from previously uncut fabric.

‡ Cut these strips from the remainder of the first or second strip cut in that color. Refer to "Cutting" below.

Amish-color center square, then repeat the color in the basket blocks.

A wide black border frames this quilt and intensifies the colors. To make a quilt similar to the one shown, select a color-splashed batik or other mottled fabric, then choose two solids, one that matches or blends with a color in the batik and another that contrasts with all colors in the batik.

To help develop your own unique color scheme for the quilt, photocopy the **Color Plan** on page 13, and use crayons or colored pencils to experiment with different color arrangements.

CUTTING

All measurements include ¼-inch seam allowances. All pieces are cut using rotary-cutting techniques. Referring to the Cutting Chart, cut the required number of strips in the width needed for your size quilt. Cut all strips across the fabric width unless otherwise indicated. From these strips, cut the individual pieces according to the instructions below. Because of the complexity of the cutting layouts, refer frequently to the **Cutting Diagrams** for guidance when cutting strips and pieces.

Since all the baskets are made from the same fabrics, the grid technique is the most efficient method to use to construct the triangle squares for the basket handles. For details on this method, see "Method 1: Grids" on page 107. If you would prefer to cut and piece the batik and red triangle squares traditionally, cut your fabric into 1⅞-inch strips for the wallhanging, 2⅞-inch strips for the bed topper, and 3⅞-inch strips for the king.

Note: Cut and piece one sample block before cutting all of the fabric for the quilt.

Wallhanging

Refer to the **Wallhanging Cutting Diagrams** for guidance.

Batik

• For the **center square**, cut one 10-inch square from the 10-inch batik strip.

• For the **basket handles**, cut one 12 × 18-inch rectangle from the 12-inch batik strip.

• For the **basket background**, cut two $4\frac{7}{8}$-inch squares from the $4\frac{7}{8}$-inch batik strip. Cut the squares in half diagonally to form four B triangles, as shown in **Diagram 1**.

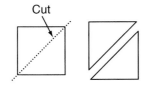

Diagram 1

Red

• For the **center triangles**, cut two $7\frac{5}{8}$-inch squares from the $7\frac{5}{8}$-inch red strip. Cut the squares in half diagonally to form four triangles.

• For the **basket handles**, cut one 12 × 18-inch rectangle from the 12-inch red strip.

• For the **basket feet**, cut four $1\frac{7}{8}$-inch squares from the $1\frac{7}{8}$-inch red strip. Cut the squares in half diagonally to form eight A triangles.

• For the **basket**, cut two $4\frac{7}{8}$-inch squares from the $4\frac{7}{8}$-inch red strip. Cut the squares in half diagonally to form four B triangles.

Purple

• For the **center triangles**, cut two $10\frac{3}{8}$-inch squares from the $10\frac{3}{8}$-inch purple strip. Cut the squares in half diagonally to form four triangles.

• For the **basket sides**, cut eight $1\frac{1}{2} × 4\frac{1}{2}$-inch rectangles from the $1\frac{1}{2}$-inch purple strips.

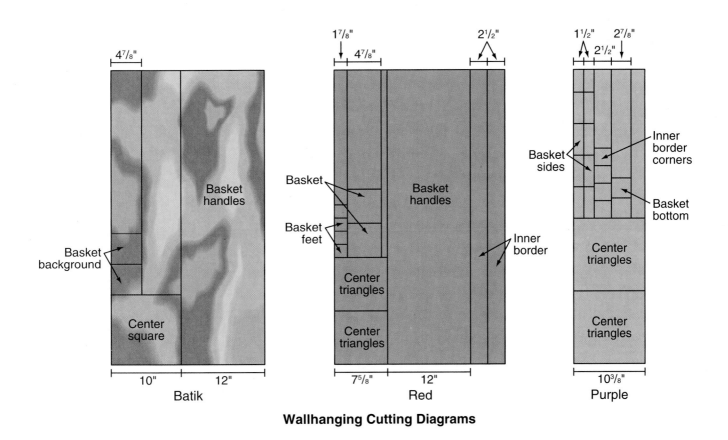

Wallhanging Cutting Diagrams

• For the **inner border corners**, cut four 2½-inch purple squares from the 2½-inch purple strip.

• For the **basket bottom**, cut two 2⅞-inch squares from the 2⅞-inch purple strip. Cut the squares in half diagonally to form four triangles.

Bed Topper

Refer to the **Bed Topper Cutting Diagrams** for guidance.

Batik

• For the **center square**, cut one 19½-inch square from the 19½-inch batik strip.

• For the **basket handles**, cut one 18 × 25-inch rectangle from the 25-inch batik strip.

• For the **basket background**, cut two 8⅞-inch squares from the 8⅞-inch batik strip. Cut the squares in half diagonally to form four B triangles, as shown in **Diagram 1** on page 5.

Red

• For the **center triangles**, cut two 14⅜-inch squares from the 14⅜-inch red strip. Cut the squares in half diagonally to form four triangles.

• For the **basket handles**, cut one 18 × 25-inch rectangle from the 25-inch red strip.

• For the **basket feet**, cut four 2⅞-inch squares from the 2⅞-inch red strip. Cut the squares in half diagonally to form eight triangles.

• For the **basket**, cut two 8⅞-inch squares from the 8⅞-inch red strip. Cut the squares in half diagonally to form four B triangles.

Purple

• For the **center triangles**, cut two 19⅞-inch squares from the 19⅞-inch purple strip. Cut the squares in half diagonally to form four triangles.

• For the **basket sides**, cut eight 2½ × 8½-inch pieces from the 2½-inch purple strips.

• For the **inner border corners**, cut four 4½-inch purple squares from the 4½-inch purple strip.

• For the **basket bottom**, cut two 4⅞-inch squares from the 4⅞-inch purple strip. Cut the squares in half diagonally to form four triangles.

King

Refer to the **King-Size Cutting Diagrams** on page 8 for guidance.

Batik

• For the **center square**, cut one 29-inch square from the 29-inch batik strip.

• For the **basket handles**, cut one 18 × 22-inch rectangle from the 22-inch batik strip.

• For the **basket background**, cut two 10⅞-inch squares from the 10⅞-inch batik strip. Cut the squares in half diagonally to form four B triangles, as shown in **Diagram 1** on page 5.

Red

• For the **center triangles**, cut two 21⅛-inch squares from the 21⅛-inch red strips. Cut the squares in half diagonally to form four triangles.

• For the **basket handles**, cut one 18 × 22-inch rectangle from the 22-inch red strip.

• For the **basket feet**, cut four 3⅜-inch squares from the 3⅜-inch red strip. Cut the squares in half diagonally to form eight A triangles.

• For the **basket**, cut two 10⅞-inch squares from the 10⅞-inch red strips. Cut the squares in half diagonally to form four B triangles.

Purple

• For the **center triangles**, cut two 29⅜-inch squares from the 29⅜-inch purple strips. Cut the squares in half diagonally to form four triangles.

• For the **basket sides**, cut eight 3½ × 10½-inch pieces from the 3½-inch purple strips.

• For the **inner border corners**, cut four 6½-inch purple squares from the 6½-inch purple strips.

• For the **basket bottom**, cut two 5⅞-inch squares from the 5⅞-inch purple strip. Cut the squares in half diagonally to form four triangles.

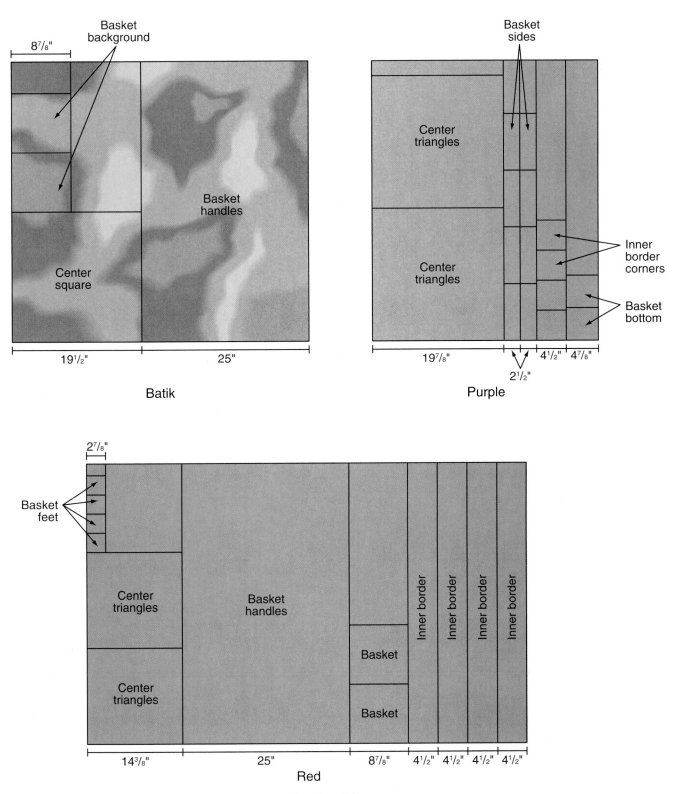

8⁷/₈"

Basket background

Basket handles

Center square

19¹/₂"

25"

Batik

Basket sides

Center triangles

Center triangles

Inner border corners

Basket bottom

19⁷/₈"

2¹/₂"

4¹/₂"

4⁷/₈"

Purple

2⁷/₈"

Basket feet

Center triangles

Center triangles

Basket handles

Basket

Basket

Inner border

Inner border

Inner border

Inner border

14³/₈"

25"

8⁷/₈"

4¹/₂"

4¹/₂"

4¹/₂"

4¹/₂"

Red

Bed Topper Cutting Diagrams

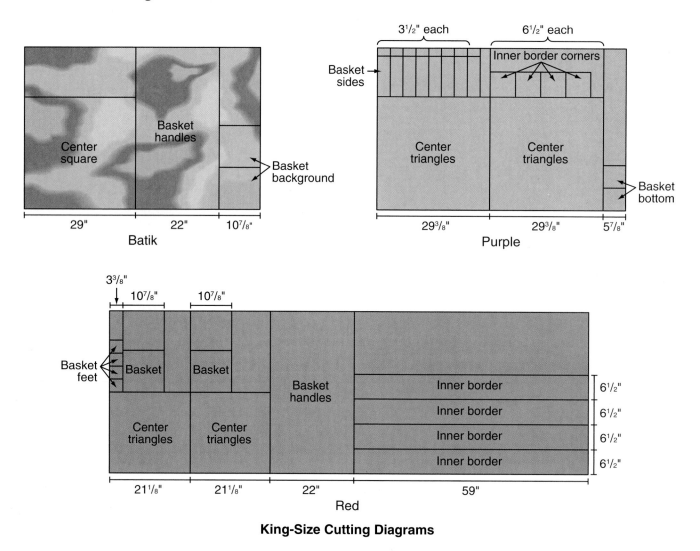

King-Size Cutting Diagrams

MAKING THE BASKET BLOCKS

The basket blocks consist of a simple pieced basket and handle, as shown in the **Block Diagram**. A total of 36 identical triangle squares are required to complete the four basket blocks, which form the corners of the outer border.

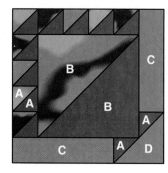

Block Diagram

Step 1. Refer to **Diagram 2** to draw and mark a triangle squares grid for each of the three sizes. To make a triangle squares grid for the wallhanging, use the 12 × 18-inch red rectangle and draw a grid of 1⅞-inch squares, eight squares across and five squares down, on the wrong side of the fabric. For the bed topper, use the 18 × 25-inch red rectangle and draw a grid of 2⅞-inch squares, eight squares across and five squares down. For the king, use the two 18 × 22-inch red rectangles and draw a grid of 3⅞-inch squares, five squares across and four squares down, on each one. Place the right sides of the fabrics together, and pair a red rectangle with a batik rectangle. Refer to the instructions on page 107 and make the triangle squares as directed. Press the seam allowance toward the red triangle in each triangle square.

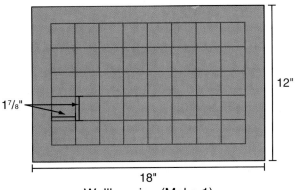

1⁷⁄₈"

18"
Wallhanging (Make 1)

12"

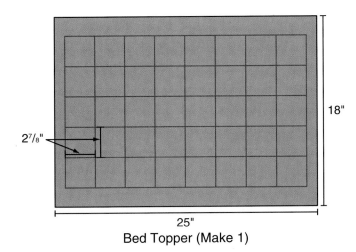

2⁷⁄₈"

25"
Bed Topper (Make 1)

18"

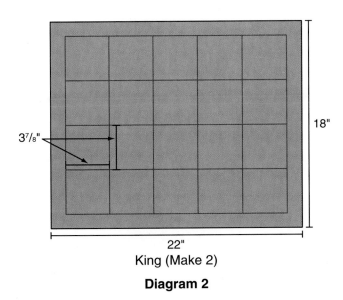

3⁷⁄₈"

22"
King (Make 2)

18"

Diagram 2

Step 2. Sew five triangle squares together as one unit and four triangle squares together as a second unit, as shown in **Diagram 3**. Press the seams toward the red triangles.

Diagram 3

Step 3. Each basket block requires two B triangles—one batik and one red. Sew the short triangle square unit to the batik B triangle, as shown in **Diagram 4**. Press the seam toward the batik. Then sew the longer triangle square unit to the batik triangle as shown, matching seams where the triangle squares meet. Press the seam toward the batik fabric.

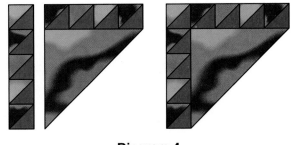

Diagram 4

Step 4. Sew the red B triangle to the bottom of the unit, as shown in **Diagram 5**. Press the seam toward the batik triangle.

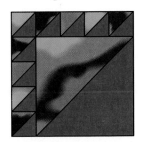

Diagram 5

Step 5. Sew a red A triangle to one end of a purple C rectangle, pressing the seam toward the rectangle. Repeat. The resulting units should be mirror images of each other, as shown in **Diagram 6** on page 10.

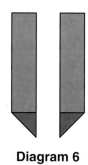

Diagram 6

Step 6. Sew an A/C unit from Step 5 to each side of the basket block, as shown in **Diagram 7**. Align the outer edges of the block with the end of the unit. Press seams toward the rectangles.

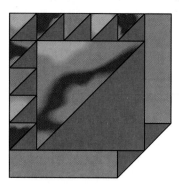

Diagram 7

Step 7. Fold a purple D triangle in half and finger press to mark the center point of its longest side. Be careful not to stretch this edge, because it is cut on the bias. Align the crease with the point of the basket and sew the two together, as shown in **Diagram 8**. Press the seam toward the D triangle. Repeat to assemble the remaining three basket blocks.

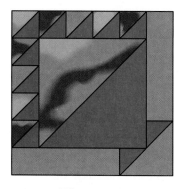

Diagram 8

ASSEMBLING THE QUILT

Step 1. Fold the batik center square in half horizontally, then vertically, to find the midpoint of each of its sides.

Step 2. Fold the red and purple center triangles in half to find the midpoints of their longest sides.

Step 3. Sew a red center triangle to each side of the batik center square, as shown in **Diagram 9**. Match the midpoints of each piece carefully, as indicated by the dashed lines in the diagram. Press the seams toward the red triangles.

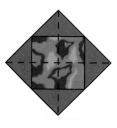

Diagram 9

Sew Easy

When adding triangles to a center square or block, sew the first two triangles to opposite sides of the square instead of adding them in a clockwise direction. This makes it easier to center the remaining triangles as they're added.

Step 4. Sew a purple center triangle to each side of the center unit, as shown in **Diagram 10**. Match midpoints carefully, and press the seams toward the purple triangles.

Diagram 10

ADDING THE BORDERS

Each border in this quilt has corner squares. The inner border features solid squares, and the outer border uses pieced blocks.

Step 1. To determine the length needed for the side borders, measure the quilt top vertically through the center. Cut two red inner borders this exact length for the sides. Measure the quilt top horizontally through the center. Cut two red inner borders this exact length for the top and bottom.

······ Sew Quick ·······

When you measure your quilt, your horizontal and vertical measurements should be the same, since the quilt is a square. However, don't rush to pick up your seam ripper and resew if the measurements vary slightly. Slight measurement differences can be corrected by carefully pressing the blocks to make sure no width is being lost in the loft of seams.

Step 2. Sew a purple inner border corner square to each end of the two top and bottom inner borders, as shown in **Diagram 11.** Press the seams toward the red border strips.

Diagram 11

Step 3. Sew on the side segments first. Fold an inner border strip in half crosswise and crease it. Unfold it and position it right side down along one side of the quilt, with the crease at the horizontal midpoint. Pin at the midpoint and ends first, then along the length of the entire side, easing in fullness as necessary. Sew it to the quilt, then repeat on the opposite side, as shown in **Diagram 12A.** Press the seams toward the border.

Sew the assembled border units to the top and bottom of the quilt in the same way that you attached the side borders, as shown in **12B.**

Match seams at corners

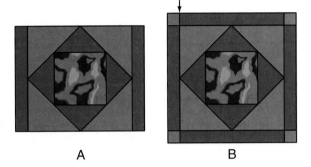

A   B

Diagram 12

Step 4. To determine the length of fabric needed for the outer borders, measure the quilt top vertically through the center, including inner borders. Using the $6\frac{1}{2}$-inch black border strips, cut a piece this exact length. Attach the pieced basket blocks for the inner border corners to the ends of two of these border pieces. Repeat Steps 1, 2, and 3 for the outer border, using the $6\frac{1}{2}$-inch black border strips. Substitute the pieced basket blocks for the inner border corners and position the baskets with their bottoms at the outer corners of the border units, as shown in **Diagram 13.**

Diagram 13

QUILTING AND FINISHING

Step 1. Mark the quilt top for quilting. In the quilt shown in the photograph on page 2, crosshatching was used in the purple center triangles, while a combination of traditional medallion, cable, floral, and scroll motifs were used elsewhere in the quilt. A winding feather pattern was quilted

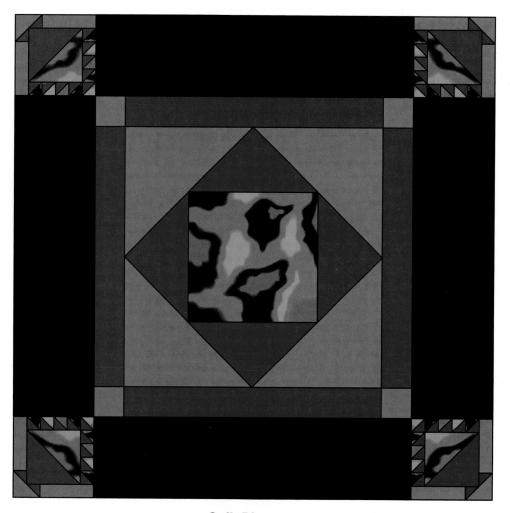

Quilt Diagram

in the outer border and a fanciful feather spray was used in the triangles.

Step 2. The backing for the wallhanging is made from a single piece of 42-inch-wide fabric, as shown in **Diagram 14**. Trim the selvages and press the 1¼-yard length of backing fabric. For the bed topper, cut the backing crosswise into two equal lengths. Trim the selvages. Cut one piece in half lengthwise, and sew a narrow panel to each side of the full-width piece. Press the seams open. For the king, cut the backing crosswise into three equal lengths. Trim the selvages. Cut 36-inch-wide panels from two of the lengths, then sew one panel to each side of the full-width panel. Press the seams open.

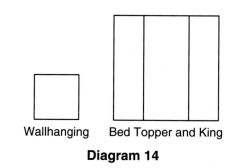

Wallhanging   Bed Topper and King

Diagram 14

Step 3. Layer the quilt top, batting, and backing, and baste the layers together. Quilt as desired.

Step 4. Refer to page 121 to make and attach double-fold binding. To calculate the amount of binding needed for your quilt, add the length of the four sides of the quilt, plus 9 inches.

AMISH HOMAGE
Color Plan

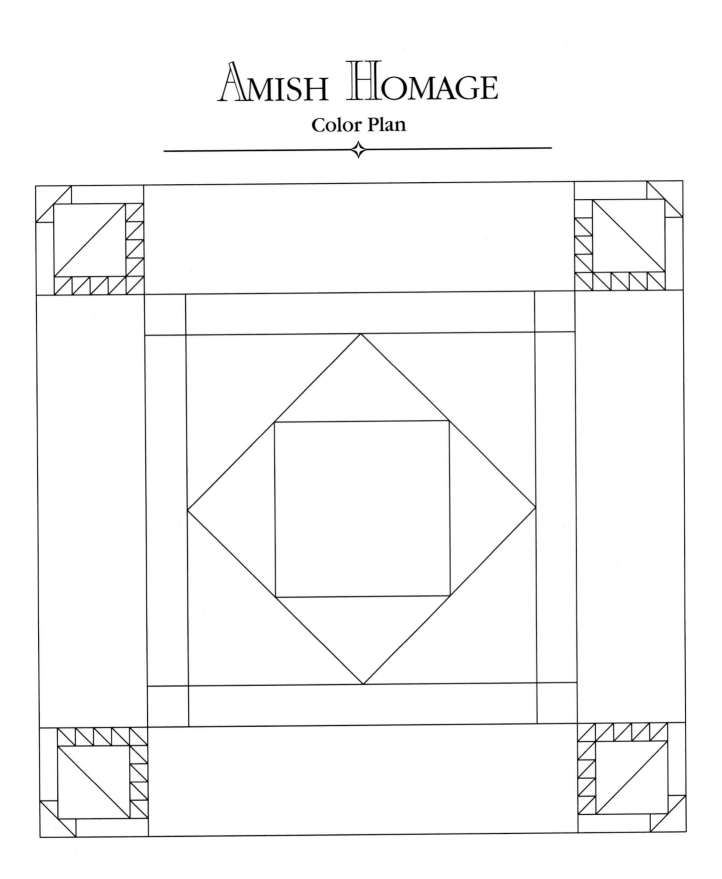

Photocopy this page and use it to experiment with color schemes for your quilt.

81 Patch

Skill Level: *Easy*

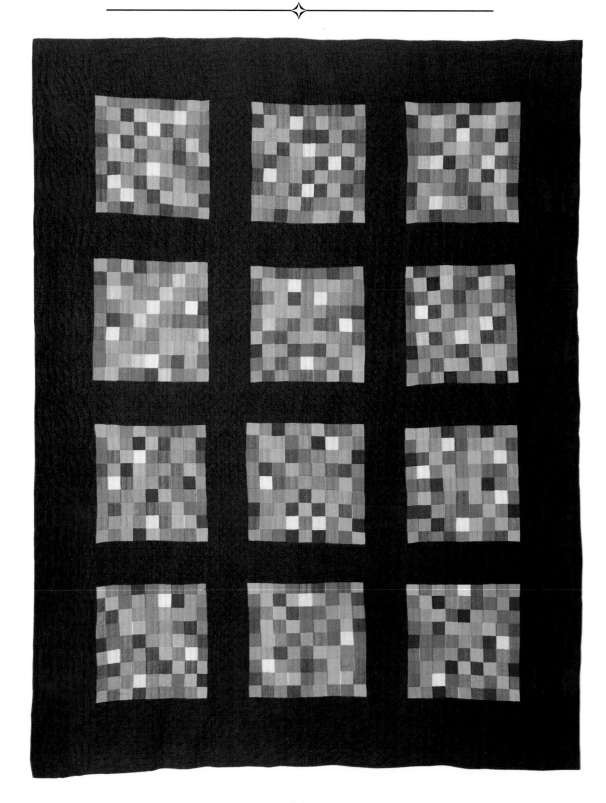

*T*he jewel-tone fabrics in this antique quilt sparkle like sunbeams through a stained glass window. From the collection of Shelly Zegart, the twin-size, 81 Patch design was pieced during the 1930s in the Amish community of Holmes County, Ohio. While the quiltmaker is unknown, there's no doubt that she dug deep into her scrap bag to find the crisp, brilliant solids for the multicolor blocks.

BEFORE YOU BEGIN

Each block in this quilt contains eighty-one 1½-inch finished squares. The 81 Patch blocks are joined by sashing strips, then finished with a wide border. All of the components of this quilt are cut and assembled using quick-cutting and quick-piecing techniques. The directions for the blocks are written based on using an easy strip-piecing method. Strips of fabric are sewn together into strip sets, and the strip sets are then cut apart and resewn into blocks. For information on rotary cutting, see page 115.

CHOOSING FABRICS

Subtle yet sparkling, the colors of the squares that crisscross through each block remain the same from block to block. From the top right corner to the lower left corner, you'll find medium blue squares. Medium pink squares are used on the opposite diagonal, stopping only for the blue square at the block's center. All other colors are placed randomly within the block.

To re-create the quilt shown, choose a medium pink solid for the squares of one diagonal and a medium blue solid for the other. Select an assortment of light to dark solids for the remaining squares in the block. The majority of fabrics in the quilt are of a medium value, with lights and darks sprinkled throughout. The quick-piecing instructions are written to allow the use of smaller yardages of fabric for the 81 Patch blocks. Purchasing fat quarters (18 × 22 inches) or fat eighths (11 × 18 inches) is a good way to increase the number of different colors used without investing in a tremendous amount of fabric.

To help develop your own unique color scheme for the

Quilt Sizes

	Twin (shown)	Queen	King
Finished Quilt Size	67" × 85½"	85½" × 104"	104" × 104"
Finished Block Size	13½"	13½"	13½"
Finished Square Size	1½"	1½"	1½"
Number of Blocks	12	20	25

Materials

	Twin	Queen	King
Black	2⅞ yards	4¼ yards	5 yards
Assorted mediums	2 yards	2⅜ yards	2⅜ yards
Assorted darks	1 yard	1¼ yards	1⅜ yards
Assorted lights	1 yard	1¼ yards	1⅜ yards
Medium blue	½ yard	⅝ yard	⅞ yard
Medium pink	½ yard	⅝ yard	⅝ yard
Backing	5¼ yards	7¾ yards	9⅜ yards
Batting	73" × 91"	91" × 110"	110" × 110"
Binding	⅝ yard	¾ yard	⅞ yard

NOTE: *Yardages are based on 44/45-inch-wide fabrics that are at least 42 inches wide after preshrinking.*

Cutting Chart

Fabric	Used For	Strip Width	Number to Cut		
			Twin	Queen	King
Black	Horizontal sashing	5½"	3	6	7
	Vertical sashing	5½"	4	7	9
	Border	8¼"	7	9	10
Assorted mediums	Strip sets*	2"	25	30	41
Assorted darks	Strip sets*	2"	13	18	22
Assorted lights	Strip sets*	2"	13	18	22
Medium blue	Strip sets*	2"	7	9	12
Medium pink	Strip sets*	2"	6	8	10

Double the number you cut if you're using fat quarters or fat eighths of fabric instead of 42-inch-wide fabric.

quilt, photocopy the **Color Plan** on page 21, and use crayons or colored pencils to experiment with different color arrangements.

CUTTING

All measurements include ¼-inch seam allowances. Referring to the Cutting Chart, cut the required number of strips in the width needed. Cut all strips across the fabric width. When you have cut the number of strips listed in the Cutting Chart, refer to the following instructions to cut the individual pieces.

• If you are using 42-inch-wide fabric, cut the 2-inch strips in half so they are approximately 21 inches long.

• If you are using fat quarters or fat eighths, cut the strips across the width of the fabric (11- or 22-inch measurement), not along the length of the fabric (9- or 18-inch measurement).

•For the horizontal sashing, cut the 5½-inch strips into 5½ × 14-inch rectangles.

ASSEMBLING THE BLOCKS

Each block in this quilt is assembled using a combination of five different strip sets. Strip sets 1 through 5 are assembled in rows first, then strip

sets 1 through 4 are added in the reverse order and turned 180 degrees to continue the medium pink and medium blue diagonal design, as shown in the **Block Diagram.**

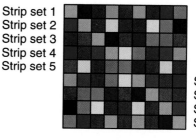

Strip set 1
Strip set 2
Strip set 3
Strip set 4
Strip set 5

Strip set 4 turned 180°
Strip set 3 turned 180°
Strip set 2 turned 180°
Strip set 1 turned 180°

Block Diagram

The following charts show how many of each strip set to make and how many segments to cut from each strip set for each quilt size.

	Number of 21-inch Strip Sets to Piece		
	Twin	Queen	King
Strip set 1	3	4	5
Strip set 2	3	4	5
Strip set 3	3	4	5
Strip set 4	3	4	5
Strip set 5	2	2	3

	Number of Segments to Cut		
	Twin	Queen	King
Strip set 1	24	40	50
Strip set 2	24	40	50
Strip set 3	24	40	50
Strip set 4	24	40	50
Strip set 5	12	20	25

Step 1. Sort the strips cut for the blocks, keeping the medium pink and medium blue strips separate. Sort the remaining strips into piles of lights, mediums, and darks.

Step 2. Make strip set 1 by sewing nine strips together lengthwise, beginning with a medium pink strip and ending with a medium blue strip, as shown in **Diagram 1**. Choose other strips from your assortment of colors and values. Position strips so all adjoining fabrics are of a different value or color. Your strip ends may be uneven due to shrinkage after prewashing. Press the seams in the direction of the arrow in the diagram.

Square off one end of each strip set.

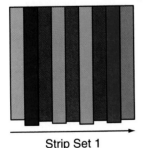

Strip Set 1

Diagram 1

Step 3. Use your rotary equipment to square up one end of the strip set, then cut as many 2-inch-wide segments from it as you can, as shown in **Diagram 2**. Set the cut strips aside. Duplicate strip set 1 until you have the total number required for your quilt size. For better color variety, use a different combination of fabrics for the assorted strips in each strip set 1, but keep the medium pink and medium blue strips in the same position. If it is necessary to use the same fabrics for each block, vary their positions in each set.

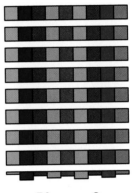

Diagram 2

Step 4. Make strip sets 2 through 5 in the same manner, paying close attention to the position of medium pink and medium blue strips, as shown in **Diagram 3** on page 18. Choose and arrange all of the other colors randomly. Press the seams in each set in the direction of the arrow in the diagram. Cut the assembled sets into 2-inch-wide segments and repeat until you have the number of segments required for your quilt. Stack segments in piles by strip set number and label them.

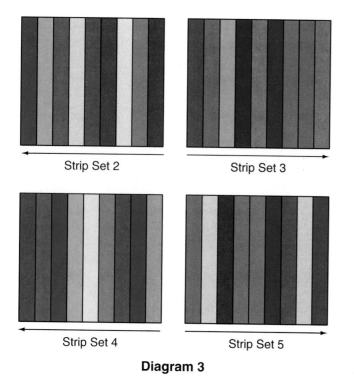

Diagram 3

Assembly Diagram

Step 5. Select two 2-inch-wide segments each from strip sets 1 through 4, and one segment from strip set 5. Referring to the **Block Diagram** on page 16, position the strip sets together to form a block. Sew the rows together, taking care to match the seams.

ASSEMBLING THE QUILT TOP

Step 1. Use a flat surface to arrange the blocks, short horizontal sashing strips, and long vertical sashing strips, as shown in the **Assembly Diagram.** The twin-size quilt has three vertical rows of four blocks each. The queen-size quilt has four vertical rows of five blocks each. The king-size quilt has five vertical rows of five blocks each.

Step 2. Sew together the columns of blocks and short sashing strips. To add a sashing strip, fold it in half crosswise and crease. Unfold it and position it right side down along the bottom of the first block, matching the crease to the vertical center of the block. Pin at the midpoint and ends, and place additional pins along the width as

necessary, easing in fullness as necessary. Sew the sashing to the block. Press the seam toward the sashing. Repeat for all of the blocks and sashing strips.

Step 3. Sew the vertical sashing to the columns. Fold the first long sashing strip in half crosswise and crease. Repeat for the first column of blocks. Match the midpoints, pinning at the center and ends first, then along the length of the entire sashing, easing in fullness as necessary. Sew the sashing strips to the blocks, taking care to align them so that your 81 Patch blocks align on both sides of a vertical sashing strip. Press the seam toward the sashing. Repeat for all remaining rows of blocks and vertical sashing strips.

ATTACHING THE BORDERS

Step 1. Attach the top and bottom borders first. Measure the width of the quilt top, taking the measurement through the horizontal center of the quilt, rather than along the edges. Sew the 8¼-inch black strips together end to end to make two borders this exact length.

Step 2. Fold one strip in half crosswise and crease. Unfold it and position it right side down along the top of the quilt, with the crease at the vertical midpoint. Pin at the midpoint and ends first, then along the length of the entire edge, easing in fullness as necessary. Sew the border to

the quilt. Repeat for the bottom border. Press seams toward the borders.

Step 3. Measure the length of the quilt top, taking the measurement through the vertical center of the quilt and including the top and bottom borders. Using the remaining black strips, piece two border strips this exact length and sew these to the sides of the quilt, referring to Step 2. Press seams toward the borders.

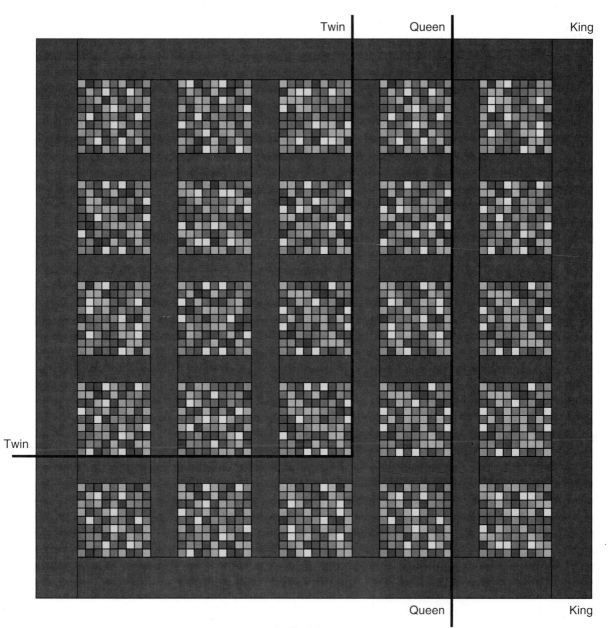

Quilt Diagram

QUILTING AND FINISHING

Step 1. Mark the quilt top for quilting. The quilt shown on page 14 features a cable motif in the border and cross-hatching in the black sashing. Vertical lines were quilted in the ditch in each block.

Step 2. To make the backing for the twin-size quilt, cut the backing fabric in half crosswise and trim the selvages. Cut two 16-inch-wide segments from the entire length of one of the pieces, and sew one segment to each side of the full-width piece, as shown in **Diagram 4**. Press the seams open.

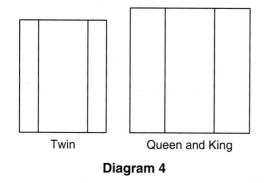

Twin   Queen and King

Diagram 4

Step 3. To make the backing for the queen-size quilt, cut the backing fabric crosswise into three equal pieces and trim the selvages. Cut a 26-inch-wide segment from the entire length of two of the pieces. Sew one segment to each side of the full-width piece, as shown in the diagram. Press the seams open.

Step 4. To make the backing for the king-size quilt, cut the backing fabric crosswise into three equal pieces and trim the selvages. Cut a 35-inch-wide segment from the entire length of two of the pieces. Sew one segment to each side of the full-width piece, as shown in the diagram. Press the seams open.

Step 5. Layer the quilt top, batting, and backing, and baste the layers together. Quilt as desired.

Step 6. Referring to the directions on page 121, make and attach double-fold binding. To calculate the amount of binding needed for the quilt size you are making, add the length of the four sides of the quilt, plus 9 inches.

81 Patch

Color Plan

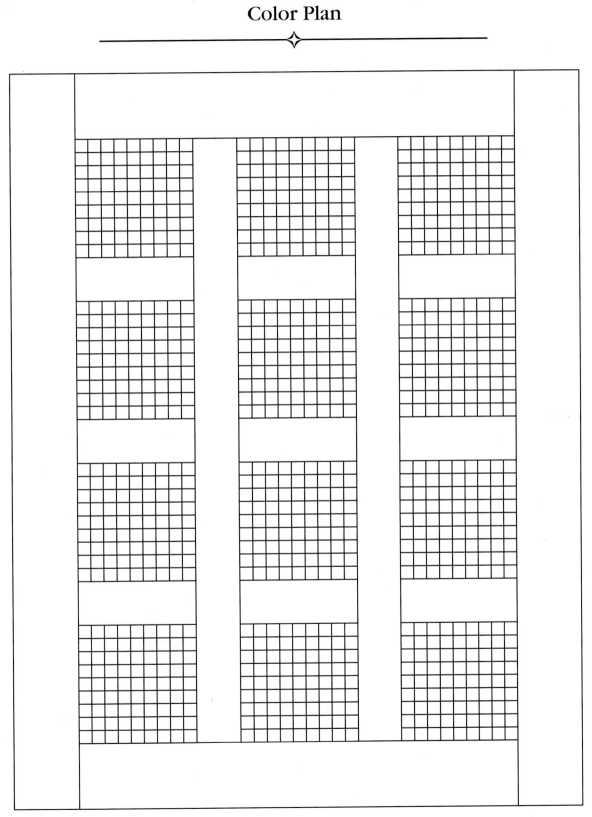

Photocopy this page and use it to experiment with color schemes for your quilt.

SPLIT BARS

O ne of the easiest patterns to piece, the bars design shown here is also one of the most striking examples of Amish style. The pattern echoes the precisely furrowed fields that typify an Amish farmer's land. Art teacher and quilt designer Stan Book of Upland, California, designed this study of color interaction as he pieced it, working from the center out. The open areas of the bars and the wide outer border allow space for showing off elaborate quilting skills.

BEFORE YOU BEGIN

Bars have long been a favorite quilt pattern of the Pennsylvania Amish. Most are designed with either five, seven, or nine vertical bars, and the center panel is usually surrounded by a narrow inner border and a wide outer border. This quilt is a variation of the bar pattern called a Split Bar quilt, since the quiltmaker chose to "split" five of the solid bars into pieced bars, each containing a middle bar of the same fabric. Adding bars to increase the quilt's size would deviate from the intended look of the design. Instead, the cutting dimensions of the bars have been increased to accommodate the larger quilt sizes.

CHOOSING FABRICS

This quilt is sewn primarily with dark, cool colors, but the quiltmaker added an element of warmth by using wine and magenta in the three center split bar units. The solid bars are a deep royal blue, just slightly lighter than the blue used in the outer border.

To help develop your own unique color scheme for the quilt, photocopy the **Color Plan** on page 27, and use crayons or colored pencils to experiment with different color arrangements. **Diagram 1** illustrates a few options for color and value placement.

Quilt Sizes

	Wallhanging	Lap (shown)	King
Finished Quilt Size	31¼" × 31¼"	52¾" × 52¾"	102" × 102"

Materials

	Wallhanging	Lap	King
Dark royal blue	½ yard	1 yard	4 yards
Royal blue	¼ yard	⅝ yard	1⅞ yards
Slate gray	¼ yard	⅜ yard	1¼ yards
Light teal	¼ yard	⅜ yard	⅞ yard
Teal	⅛ yard	⅛ yard	⅜ yard
Dark magenta	⅛ yard	⅛ yard	⅜ yard
Magenta	⅛ yard	⅛ yard	⅜ yard
Wine	⅛ yard	⅛ yard	⅜ yard
Forest green	⅛ yard	⅛ yard	⅜ yard
Backing	1⅛ yards	3½ yards	9⅜ yards
Batting	38" × 38"	59" × 59"	108" × 108"
Binding	⅜ yard	⅞ yard	1 yard

NOTE: *Yardages are based on 44/45-inch-wide fabrics that are at least 42 inches wide after preshrinking.*

CUTTING

All measurements include ¼-inch seam allowances. Although this is a simple pattern to assemble, accurate measuring and cutting are essential. Be sure to verify piece sizes as you work.

Cutting Chart

Fabric	Used For	Wallhanging		Lap		King	
		Strip Width	Number of Strips	Strip Width	Number of Strips	Strip Width	Number of Strips
Dark royal blue	Outer border	4½"	3	7¾"	4	13½"	10
Royal blue	Wide bars	2¾"	2	4¼"	4	8"	7
Slate gray	Inner border	1¾"	3	2½"	4	4½"	8
Light teal	Center bars	1¼"	3	1¾"	5	3"	7
Teal	Narrow bars	1¼"	1	1¾"	2	3"	4
Dark magenta	Narrow bars	1¼"	1	1¾"	2	3"	4
Magenta	Narrow bars	1¼"	1	1¾"	2	3"	4
Wine	Narrow bars	1¼"	1.	1¾"	2	3"	4
Forest green	Narrow bars	1¼"	1	1¾"	2	3"	4

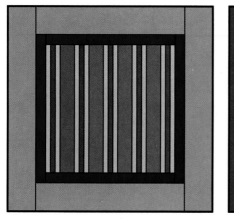
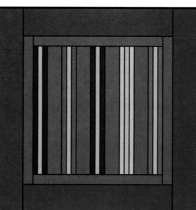
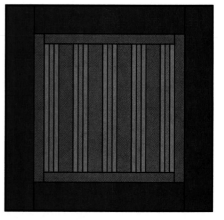

Diagram 1

SEWING THE BARS

Step 1. The assortment of narrow strips is used to assemble the split bar units. The wider, royal blue strips become the bars that separate them. Trim the wallhanging strips to 20¾ inches and the lap strips to 34¼ inches. For the king-size quilt, piece strips of like width and color together end to end, then cut them into 68-inch strips.

Step 2. To make the first split bar unit, sew a narrow teal strip to each side of a light teal strip, as shown in **Diagram 2**. Match and pin the strip edges carefully. Press the seams toward the outer strips. Referring to the diagram, repeat with all re-maining narrow strips. Sew matching narrow strips of dark magenta, magenta, wine, and forest green to each side of the four remaining light teal strips.

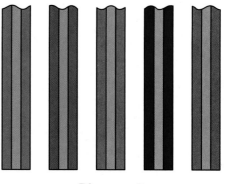

Diagram 2

·········Sew Quick·········

To keep the long strips of fabric from slipping when sewing, place one strip face down on top of the other and press them before you sew. Fabrics that are 100 percent cotton will "stick" to each other, reducing the tendency of long strips to slip and slide.

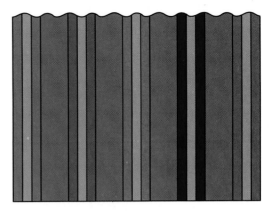

Diagram 3

Step 3. Use a flat surface to arrange the split bar units and the royal blue solid bars, beginning and ending with a split bar unit, as shown in **Diagram 3**. In the quilt shown on page 22, the split bars containing warm colors are positioned in the central portion of the quilt. Sew all bars together lengthwise, matching edges carefully and pinning as needed to hold the fabric in place. Press all seams toward the split bar units.

ADDING THE BORDERS

Step 1. Referring to the **Quilt Diagram,** sew on the top and bottom inner borders first. Measure the width of the quilt top, taking the measurement through the horizontal center of the quilt rather than along the edges. Trim two slate gray border strips to this exact length. For the king-size quilt,

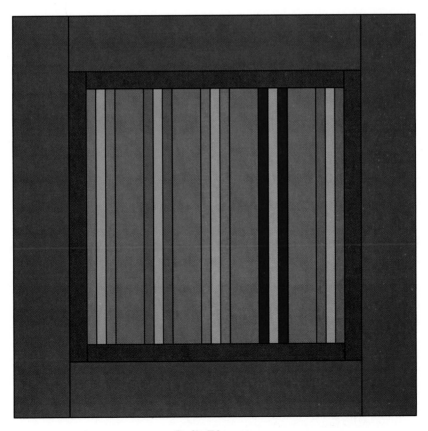

Quilt Diagram

sew strips end to end and trim to the correct length. Press all seams in one direction.

Step 2. Fold one strip in half crosswise and crease. Unfold it and position it right sides together along the top of the quilt, with the crease at the midpoint. Pin at the midpoint and ends first, then along the length of the entire border, easing in fullness as necessary. Sew the border to the quilt. Repeat on the bottom of the quilt.

Step 3. Measure the length of the quilt, taking the measurement through the vertical center of the quilt and including the top and bottom borders. Use the remaining slate gray strips to cut two border strips this exact length. For the king-size quilt, sew strips together end to end and trim to the correct length. Press all seams in one direction.

Step 4. In the same manner that the top and bottom borders were added in Step 2, pin and sew the borders to the sides of the quilt.

Step 5. To add the outer border strips, refer to Steps 1 through 4 and measure the width and length of the quilt for correct border lengths. Sew the top and bottom outer borders to the quilt before attaching the side borders. Sew strips together end to end where longer lengths are necessary.

QUILTING AND FINISHING

Step 1. Mark the quilt top for quilting. The simplicity of a bar quilt's design allows you to showcase your quilting talents. A variety of motifs were used in the quilt shown in the photograph on page 22. The two outer segments of the split bar units were quilted with vertical lines, while a

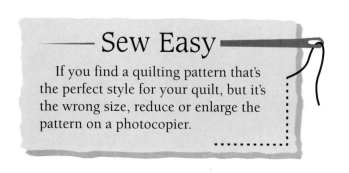

Sew Easy

If you find a quilting pattern that's the perfect style for your quilt, but it's the wrong size, reduce or enlarge the pattern on a photocopier.

cable design was used in each center bar. A cross-hatch pattern was quilted in the royal blue bars. The inner border was quilted with a double cross-hatch design, and a leafy vine winds itself around the outer border.

Step 2. To make the backing for the wall-hanging, trim the selvages and cut a 39-inch square from the backing fabric, as shown in **Diagram 4.**

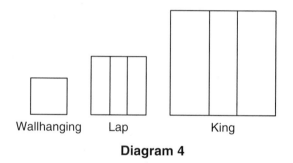

Wallhanging   Lap   King

Diagram 4

Step 3. For the lap quilt, cut the backing fabric crosswise into two equal pieces and trim the selvages. Cut one piece in half lengthwise. Cut a 19-inch-wide segment from the entire length of the remaining piece, then sew one of the wider pieces to each side of it, as shown in the diagram. Press the seams open.

Step 4. For the king-size quilt, cut the backing fabric crosswise into three equal pieces and trim the selvages. Cut a 30-inch-wide segment from the entire length of one piece, then sew one of the wider pieces to each side of it, as shown in the diagram. Press the seams open.

Step 5. Layer the quilt top, batting, and backing. Baste the layers together and quilt as desired.

Step 6. Referring to the directions on page 121, make and attach double-fold binding to finish at a width of ¼ inch for the wallhanging. Binding for both the lap and king-size quilts should finish at a width of ½ inch, so binding strips should be cut 2½ inches wide for these quilt sizes. To calculate the amount of binding needed for the quilt size you are making, add up the length of the four sides of the quilt, plus 9 inches.

SPLIT BARS

Color Plan

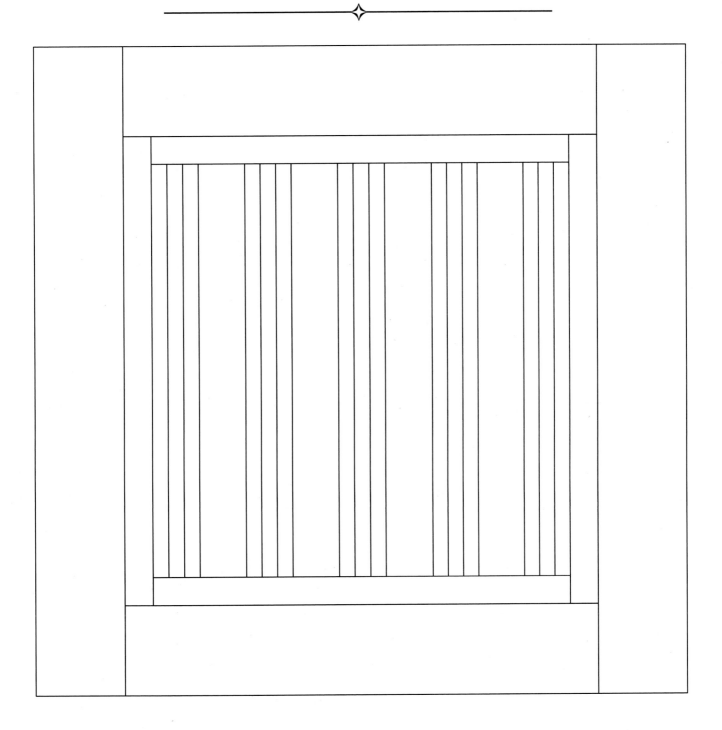

Photocopy this page and use it to experiment with color schemes for your quilt.

DOUBLE IRISH CHAIN

Skill Level: *Easy*

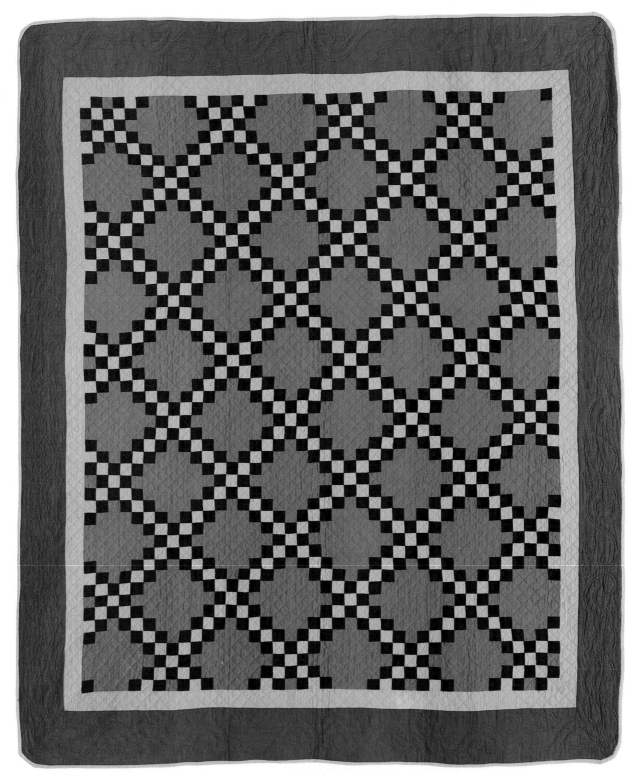

*W*hile not unique to Amish quiltmakers, the Double Irish Chain pattern has been lovingly adopted and circulated among Amish communities, particularly in the Midwest. This 1930s quilt is owned by quilt collector Bryce Hamilton of Minneapolis, Minnesota. The color scheme may be simple, but the effect is stunning. The clear, sharp lines of diagonal "chains" frame the areas of solid color, leaving ample room to showcase fine quilting.

BEFORE YOU BEGIN

This quilt is assembled by alternating two quick-pieced blocks. Four different strip sets are rotary cut and sewn together, then short segments are cut from each to create a block.

Notice that the quilt in the photograph is not symmetrical. While this lack of symmetry adds a charming touch, these instructions are written so that the design is complete on all sides. Also, the Amish did not usually miter their borders since mitering requires more fabric. We've changed the original quilt design to feature straight borders instead of mitered ones to reflect this time-honored Amish tradition.

CHOOSING FABRICS

To make a quilt similar to the one shown in the photograph on the opposite page, choose a royal blue solid for the background and a slightly darker shade of the same blue for the border. For the chains, you'll need black and mint green solids. Since only three colors are used to construct the Double Irish Chain pattern, feel free to substitute other recognizably Amish colors (like purple, pink, and forest green) for the royal blue, black, and mint green fabrics to create a different effect in your own quilt. To help develop your own unique color scheme for the quilt, photocopy the **Color Plan** on page 35, and use colored pencils or markers to experiment with different color arrangements.

Quilt Sizes

	Twin (shown)	Queen	King
Finished Quilt Size	$72\frac{3}{4}" \times 85\frac{1}{4}"$	$85\frac{1}{4}" \times 97\frac{3}{4}"$	$97\frac{3}{4}" \times 97\frac{3}{4}"$
Finished Block Size			
A Blocks	$6\frac{1}{4}"$	$6\frac{1}{4}"$	$6\frac{1}{4}"$
B Blocks	$6\frac{1}{4}"$	$6\frac{1}{4}"$	$6\frac{1}{4}"$
Number of Blocks			
A Blocks	50	72	85
B Blocks	49	71	84

Materials

	Twin	Queen	King
Royal blue	$2\frac{5}{8}$ yards	$3\frac{3}{8}$ yards	4 yards
Black	$2\frac{3}{8}$ yards	3 yards	$3\frac{1}{2}$ yards
Mint green	$1\frac{7}{8}$ yards	$2\frac{3}{8}$ yards	$2\frac{5}{8}$ yards
Dark royal blue	$1\frac{3}{8}$ yards	$1\frac{3}{4}$ yards	$1\frac{3}{4}$ yards
Backing	$5\frac{1}{4}$ yards	$7\frac{7}{8}$ yards	9 yards
Batting	$79" \times 92"$	$92" \times 104"$	$104" \times 104"$
Binding	$\frac{3}{4}$ yard	$\frac{3}{4}$ yard	$\frac{3}{4}$ yard

NOTE: Yardages are based on 44/45-inch-wide fabrics that are at least 42 inches wide after preshrinking.

29

Cutting Chart

Fabric	Used For	Strip Width	Number to Cut		
			Twin	Queen	King
Royal blue	Strip sets 1 and 3	1¾"	11	15	18
	Strip set 4	4¼"	6	7	8
	B Blocks	6¾"	6	8	10
Black	Strip sets 1, 2, 3, and 4	1¾"	43	57	66
Mint green	Strip sets 1, 2, and 3	1¾"	23	32	37
	Inner border	2½"	7	8	8
Dark royal blue	Outer border	6½"	7	9	9

CUTTING

All measurements include ¼-inch seam allowances. Referring to the Cutting Chart, cut the required number of strips for your quilt size, then refer to the instructions below to cut the individual pieces. Cut all strips across the fabric width.

From the 6¾-inch royal blue strips, cut 4¼-inch segments. You will need 49 segments for the twin, 71 for the queen, and 84 for the king.

Note: Cut and piece one sample block before cutting all of the fabric for the quilt.

MAKING THE STRIP SETS

The **Block Diagram** illustrates the two blocks used in this quilt. Block A uses three strip sets and Block B uses another type of strip set added to either side of a rectangle.

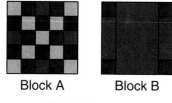

Block A   Block B

Block Diagram

Step 1. The three strip sets used to assemble Block A are shown in **Diagram 1**. Group the cut strips by strip set and label the piles by strip set number to avoid confusion.

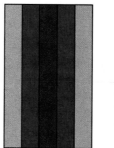

Strip Set 1   Strip Set 2   Strip Set 3

Diagram 1

········Sew Quick········

Instead of sewing together all of the strip sets before cutting any of the short segments, save time by sewing together one less strip set than is required. Then cut as many 1¾-inch segments as you can from the assembled strip sets. Determine how many more are required for your quilt size. If you only need a few more segments, you may want to make your final strip set a shorter one—just long enough to yield the needed segments.

Step 2. To make strip set 1, sew strips together lengthwise in the following order: mint green, black, royal blue, black, and mint green. Match one end of the strips carefully so there will be less waste when the set is squared up after sewing. Press all seams in the same direction. Repeat to make five of strip set 1 for the twin, seven for the queen, and eight for the king.

Step 3. Square up one end of the set, then cut as many 1¾-inch segments from it as possible, as shown in **Diagram 2**. Stack the segments together, label them, and set them aside. Repeat until you have 100 strip set 1 segments for the twin, 144 for the queen, and 170 for the king.

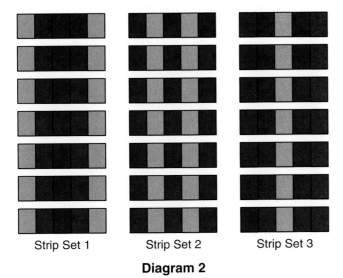

Strip Set 1   Strip Set 2   Strip Set 3

Diagram 2

Step 4. To make strip set 2, sew strips together lengthwise in the following order: black, mint green, black, mint green, and black. Press all seams in the same direction. Repeat to make five of strip set 2 for the twin, seven for the queen, and eight for the king. Square up one end of the set, then cut as many 1¾-inch segments from it as possible. Stack the segments together and repeat until you have 100 strip set 2 segments for the twin, 144 for the queen, and 170 for the king.

Step 5. To make strip set 3, sew strips together lengthwise in the following order: royal blue, black, mint green, black, and royal blue. Press all seams in the same direction. Repeat to make three of strip set 3 for the twin, four for the queen, and five for the king. Square up one end of the set,

and cut as many 1¾-inch segments from it as possible. Stack the segments together. Repeat until you have 50 strip set 3 segments for the twin, 72 for the queen, and 85 for the king.

PIECING THE BLOCKS

Step 1. To assemble Block A, position two strip set 1 segments, two strip set 2 segments, and one strip set 3 segment, as shown in **Diagram 3**, with seams facing in opposite directions. Sew the segments in each block together, matching seam intersections carefully. Press the seams away from the center segment.

Strip set 1
Strip set 2
Strip set 3
Strip set 2
Strip set 1

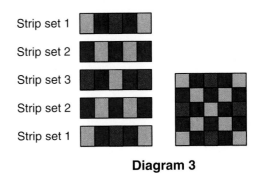

Diagram 3

Step 2. To make Block B, sew one 1¾-inch black strip to each side of a 4¼-inch royal blue strip, as shown in **Diagram 4A**. Press the seams toward the center strip. Repeat to make six of strip set 4 for the twin, seven for the queen, and eight for the king. Square up one end of the set, then cut as many 1¾-inch segments from it as possible, as shown in **4B**. Stack the segments together. Repeat until you have assembled 98 strip set 4 segments for the twin, 142 for the queen, and 168 for the king.

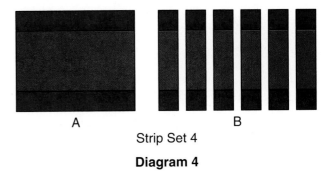

A   B

Strip Set 4

Diagram 4

Step 3. Sew a strip set 4 segment to each long side of a royal blue rectangle, as shown in **Diagram 5**. Press the seams toward the rectangle. Repeat until you have assembled the total number of B blocks required for your quilt size.

Diagram 5

— Sew Easy —

When pressing strip sets, lift your iron instead of sliding it to prevent the joined strips from warping or stretching. Press from the wrong side first to position the seam allowances correctly, then turn the assembled block over and gently glide the iron across it.

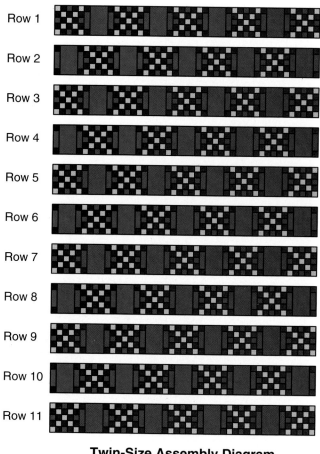

Row 1
Row 2
Row 3
Row 4
Row 5
Row 6
Row 7
Row 8
Row 9
Row 10
Row 11

Twin-Size Assembly Diagram

ASSEMBLING THE QUILT TOP

To lay out the quilt top, stagger Blocks A and B in alternate rows. All odd-numbered rows begin and end with an A block, and all even-numbered rows begin and end with a B block. Using the **Twin-Size Assembly Diagram**, lay the blocks in rows. The twin-size quilt has eleven rows, each containing nine blocks. The queen-size quilt has 13 rows, each containing 11 blocks. The king-size quilt has 13 rows, each containing 13 blocks. Sew the blocks in each row together, and press the seams toward the B blocks. To complete the top, sew the rows together. Press.

ADDING THE BORDERS

Step 1. Sew on the top and bottom inner borders first. Measure the width of the quilt top, taking the measurement through the horizontal

center of the quilt rather than along the edges. Sew 2½-inch mint green border strips end to end to get this exact length for the inner borders.

Step 2. Fold one of the strips in half crosswise and crease. Unfold it and position it right side down along the top of the quilt, with the crease at the vertical midpoint. Pin at the midpoint and ends first, then along the entire edge, easing in fullness as necessary. Sew the border to the quilt. Repeat on the bottom of the quilt.

Step 3. To assemble the side borders, measure the length of the quilt, taking the measurement through the vertical center of the quilt and including the top and bottom borders. Use the remaining mint green strips to piece two inner border strips this exact length. Sew the borders to the quilt sides in the same manner as for the top and bottom borders.

Step 4. To add the 6½-inch dark royal blue outer border strips, measure the quilt horizontally through the center and sew the royal blue strips end to end to piece two outer borders this exact length. Sew to the top and bottom of the quilt as directed in Step 2. Measure the length of the quilt top vertically through the center, then piece and add the borders to the sides of the quilt.

Step 5. If you would like your quilt to have rounded corners like the quilt shown on page 28, use a plate or other circular object to trace a gentle curve at each corner of the quilt, as shown in **Diagram 6.** Be sure the plate is in the same position for each corner so the curves will be the same size. Trim the fabric outside the marked lines.

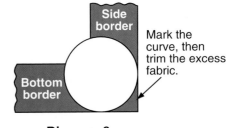

Diagram 6

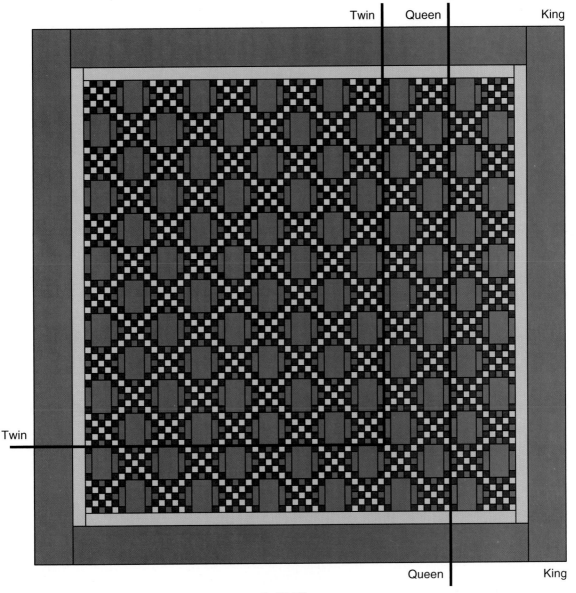

Quilt Diagram

QUILTING AND FINISHING

Step 1. Mark the quilt top for quilting. In the quilt shown on page 28, the pieced top and the inner borders were both quilted in a crosshatch pattern. A vine motif was used in the outer border.

Step 2. To make the backing for the twin quilt, cut the backing fabric in half crosswise and trim the selvages. Cut one of the pieces in half lengthwise, and sew one narrow panel to each side of the full-width piece, as shown in **Diagram 7**. Press the seams open.

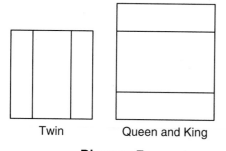

Twin   Queen and King

Diagram 7

Step 3. To make the backing for either the queen- or king-size quilt, cut the backing fabric crosswise into three equal pieces and trim the selvages. Cut 33-inch-wide panels from two of the pieces and sew one panel to each side of the full-width piece, as shown in the diagram. Press the seams open.

Step 4. Layer the quilt top, batting, and backing, and baste the layers together. Quilt as desired.

Step 5. Referring to the directions on page 121, make and attach double-fold bias binding. To calculate the amount of binding needed for the quilt size you are making, add the length of the four sides of the quilt, plus 9 inches. When attaching the binding, be sure to ease in enough fullness around the rounded corners to allow for turning the binding smoothly to the quilt back. You will need to take extra stitches around the corners to hold the binding in place.

DOUBLE IRISH CHAIN
Color Plan

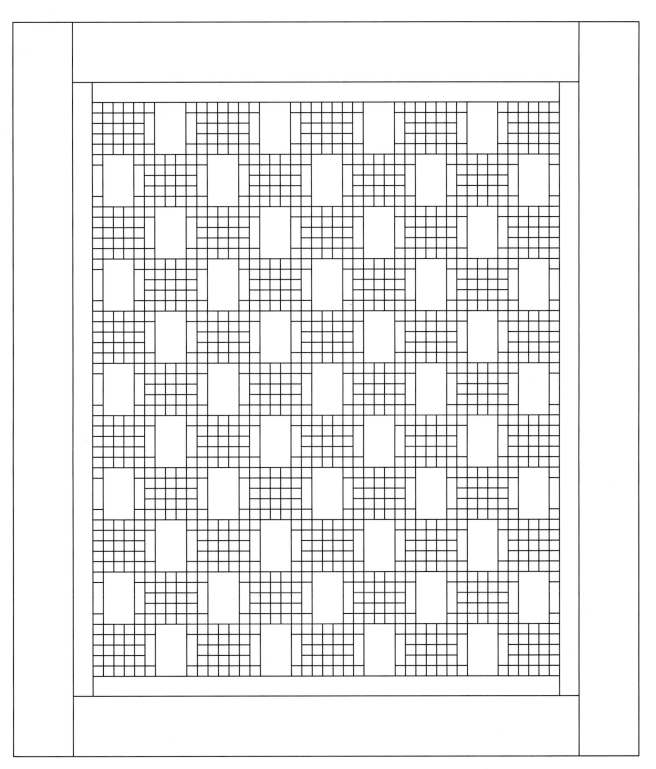

Photocopy this page and use it to experiment with color schemes for your quilt.

Broken Dishes

Skill Level: *Easy*

*T*rue to the Amish tradition of finding creative inspiration in everyday life, the Broken Dishes quilt pattern may have been named for the well-used tableware of Amish families. This wallhanging was inspired by an antique quilt featured in a country decorating magazine. Its owner, Sandy Freeman of Allentown, Pennsylvania, worked with a quiltmaker to select the perfect combination of lights, mediums, and darks to bring an old-fashioned scrappy look to this new quilt.

BEFORE YOU BEGIN

The blocks in this quilt are assembled using only one shape, a right triangle. The triangles are sewn together along their bias edges to produce half-square triangle blocks, which are arranged in groups of four to create the Broken Dishes block. If you want a random color scheme, use the single squares method on page 109 to construct the triangle squares. If you choose to make all of your blocks in either the same color scheme or from a limited color palette, use the grid technique on page 107 to construct the triangle squares.

CHOOSING FABRICS

This quilt is sewn from a variety of Amish solids, ranging from deep, rich colors to light, sparkling pastels. Yardage recommendations are based on making a quilt similar in color value to the one shown. The quiltmaker chose black, navy, dark green, and dark brown to represent the darks; rust, royal blue, teal, orchid, and medium brown to represent the mediums; and pale yellow, salmon, moss green, light green, and tan to represent the lights. Adjust the yardages for each group of colors if you plan to change the proportion of dark, medium, and light fabrics. If you are a beginning quiltmaker, a planned and possibly symmet-

Quilt Sizes

	Wallhanging (shown)	Double	King
Finished Quilt Size	72³⁄₄" × 72³⁄₄"	83³⁄₄" × 100¹⁄₄"	100¹⁄₄" × 100¹⁄₄"
Finished Block Size	5¹⁄₂"	5¹⁄₂"	5¹⁄₂"
Number of Blocks	100	180	225
Number of Triangle Squares	400	720	900

Materials

	Wallhanging	Double	King
Forest green	1⁵⁄₈ yards	1³⁄₄ yards	2¹⁄₄ yards
Assorted darks	1²⁄₃ yards	2³⁄₄ yards	3¹⁄₂ yards
Assorted mediums	1¹⁄₃ yards	2¹⁄₄ yards	2⁵⁄₈ yards
Assorted lights	1¹⁄₃ yards	2¹⁄₄ yards	2⁵⁄₈ yards
Moss green	⁵⁄₈ yard	³⁄₄ yard	³⁄₄ yard
Backing	4²⁄₃ yards	7³⁄₄ yards	9¹⁄₈ yards
Batting	79" × 79"	90" × 107"	107" × 107"
Binding	³⁄₄ yard	³⁄₄ yard	⁷⁄₈ yard

NOTE: Yardages are based on 44/45-inch-wide fabrics that are at least 42 inches wide after preshrinking.

Cutting Chart

Fabric	Used For	Strip Width	Number of Strips		
			Wallhanging	Double	King
Forest green	Outer border	7"	7	9	10
Assorted darks, mediums, and lights	Triangle squares*				
Moss green	Inner border	2½"	6	9	9

See specific cutting information for triangle squares in the text. The size of the pieces or strips you cut will depend on the cutting method you choose.

rical color scheme may work best. A more experienced quiltmaker may want to select a variety of fabric values and colors to achieve a more random look.

Before purchasing fabric, decide which quick-piecing method you will use to make the triangle squares. If you choose the grid method, be sure to purchase fabric pieces large enough to accommodate the grid you intend to draw. You may decide to use a combination of methods to make the best use of fabric you have on hand.

For a discussion of the fabrics and colors used in traditional Amish quilts, see page 106. To help develop your own unique color scheme for the quilt, photocopy the **Color Plan** on page 43, and use crayons or colored pencils to experiment with different color arrangements.

CUTTING

All measurements include ¼-inch seam allowances.

The finished size of the individual triangle squares is 2¾ inches. If you are cutting and piecing together individual triangles (which is a good way to use scraps), refer to page 109 and cut the triangles so the perpendicular or short sides are 3⅝ inches long and on the straight of grain. If you're using the sandwiched squares method, refer to page 109 and use 3⅝-inch squares of fabric. If you're using the grid method of triangle

square assembly, refer to page 107 and draw a 3⅝-inch grid on your fabric as directed.

Four triangle squares are sewn together to create one Broken Dishes block.

Note: Cut and piece one sample block before cutting all of the fabric for the quilt.

DESIGNING THE OVERALL LAYOUT

To construct a Broken Dishes block, arrange four triangle squares so they form an on-point square at the block's center, as shown in **Diagram 1A**. Two traditional options for color value placement are shown in **1B** (using lights and darks) and **1C** (using lights, mediums, and darks).

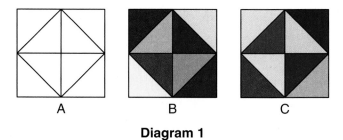

Diagram 1

Colors usually vary, but if value placement remains consistent from block to block, a diagonal pattern of flip-flopping triangle pairs is created when the blocks are sewn together, as shown in **Diagram 2**. (Refer to page 106 for information about color value.)

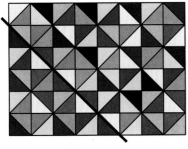

Diagram 2

In the quilt shown on page 36, the quiltmaker chose to add interest by varying the placement of color value in her blocks; this is often referred to as "sparkle" in Amish quilts. A few examples of the variations are shown in **Diagram 3**.

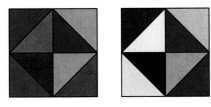

Diagram 3

Before beginning your quilt, you may find it helpful to sort all of the fabrics that you intend to use by color value.

PIECING THE BLOCKS

Step 1. Refer to the Quilt Sizes chart on page 37 for the quantity of triangle squares required for your quilt size. The majority of the Broken Dishes blocks in the quilt shown pair a light or medium triangle with a dark triangle. The amount of contrast in each pair will depend on the look you are trying to achieve. For example, to make a block similar to the one shown in **Diagram 1B,** you would sew four triangle squares with a dark/light contrast. For the block shown in **1C,** you would sew two medium/light triangle squares and two dark/light triangle squares. Use your Color Plan to determine the total number of each type required for your quilt.

— Sew Easy —

If you are using a variety of value combinations in your quilt, you'll want to experiment before you begin piecing the actual triangle squares. Make a copy of the blank color plan, then cut out and shade individual blocks with a pencil. Tape the shaded blocks onto a sheet of paper to make a mock-up of your planned quilt, and jot the number of each color value required next to the drawings. Hang the paper near your work area for a handy reference as you sew.

Step 2. Choose one of the quick-piecing methods discussed previously to assemble the required number of triangle squares. Press seams toward the darker half of each triangle square. Group triangle squares by color or value, or in some way that makes it easy to make selections as you assemble them into Broken Dishes blocks.

Step 3. Select four triangle squares. Position and sew them together in pairs of upper or lower block units, as shown in **Diagram 4A.** Refer to your Color Plan as necessary for value placement. Press seams where triangle squares meet in the center in opposite directions, then match seams carefully and sew the units together, as shown in **4B.** Do not press the final seam yet. In the same manner, assemble the total number of Broken Dishes blocks required for your quilt size.

Upper block unit

Lower block unit

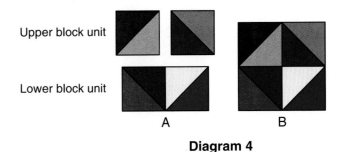

A   B

Diagram 4

Assembling the Quilt Top

Step 1. Use a design wall or other flat surface to lay out the Broken Dishes blocks. Refer to both the **Wallhanging Assembly Diagram** and your **Color Plan** when laying out the blocks for the wallhanging. The wallhanging has ten rows of Broken Dishes blocks across and ten rows down.

Note: The wallhanging shown on page 36 has a row of half-blocks at the top of the quilt, plus another at the bottom. To assemble your quilt in the same manner, make ten upper and ten lower block units, as shown in **Diagram 4A,** but do not sew the two block halves together. The wallhanging is assembled into rows containing ten whole blocks across and nine down. To complete the wallhanging, the lower block units are added to the top row, and the upper block units are added to the bottom row.

Sew Easy

If you are making a scrappy quilt, leave the room for a few minutes after you've decided on the block layout. See if the arrangement still pleases when you return. If it doesn't, keep moving the blocks and stepping away for a while until you are satisfied with the overall design.

Step 2. Refer to the **Double- and King-Size Assembly Diagram** if you are making the double- or king-size quilt. Arrange your blocks into rows and columns, referring to your Color Plan for block placement. The double-size quilt has 12 rows across and 15 rows down, and the king-size quilt has 15 rows across and 15 rows down.

Row of half blocks
(use lower block unit)

Row of Broken Dishes blocks

Row of half blocks
(use upper block unit)

Wallhanging Assembly Diagram

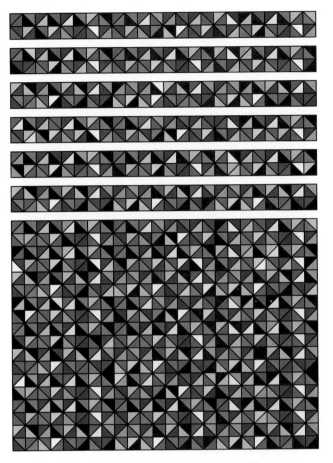

Double- and King-Size Assembly Diagram

Step 2. Fold one of the strips in half crosswise and crease. Unfold it and position it right side down along one side of the quilt, with the crease at the horizontal midpoint. Pin at the midpoint and ends first, then along the length of the entire side, easing in fullness as necessary. Sew the border to the quilt top. Repeat on the opposite side of the quilt.

Step 3. Measure the width of the quilt top, taking the measurement through the horizontal center of the quilt and including the side borders. Use your 2½-inch-wide moss green strips to assemble two border strips this exact length.

Step 4. Fold one strip in half crosswise and crease. Unfold the strip and position it right side down along the top edge of the quilt, matching the crease to the vertical midpoint. Pin at the midpoint and ends first, then across the entire width of the quilt, easing in fullness if necessary. Sew the border to the quilt. Repeat on the bottom edge of the quilt.

Step 5. Prepare and add the outer borders to the quilt in the same manner as for the inner borders, sewing on the side borders first, then the top and bottom borders.

Step 3. Before sewing the blocks together, press the center horizontal seam of adjacent blocks in opposite directions so the seams can be butted together for an accurate match. Sew the blocks together into rows.

Step 4. Sew all rows together, matching all seams carefully. Press the quilt.

ADDING THE BORDERS

Step 1. Attach the side borders to the quilt first. Measure the length of the quilt top, taking the measurement through the vertical center of the quilt rather than along the edges. Use your 2½-inch moss green strips to assemble two border strips this exact length.

QUILTING AND FINISHING

Step 1. Mark the quilt top for quilting. In the quilt shown in the photograph on page 36, the inner border was quilted with a continuous scallop design, while a series of 60-degree diamonds produces a chevron-like outline in the outer border. Each patch in the Broken Dishes blocks is outline quilted about ⅛ inch away from the seam line.

Step 2. To make the backing for the wallhanging, divide the fabric crosswise into two equal pieces, and trim the selvages. Cut one of the pieces in half lengthwise and sew one half to each side of the full-width piece, as shown in **Diagram 5** on page 42. Press the seams open.

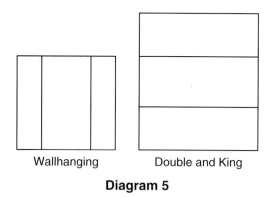

Wallhanging   Double and King

Diagram 5

Step 3. To make the backing for the double- or king-size quilt, cut the backing fabric crosswise into three equal pieces, and trim the selvages. Cut 34-inch-wide segments from two of the pieces for the double size and 38-inch-wide segments from two of the pieces for the king size. Sew one segment to each side of the full-width piece, as shown in the diagram. Press the seams open.

Step 4. Layer the quilt top, batting, and backing, and baste the layers together. Quilt as desired.

Step 5. Referring to the directions on page 121, make and attach double-fold binding to finish at a width of ⅜ inch. To calculate the amount of binding needed for the quilt size you are making, add up the length of the four sides of the quilt, plus 9 inches. Attach the binding using a ⅜-inch seam allowance.

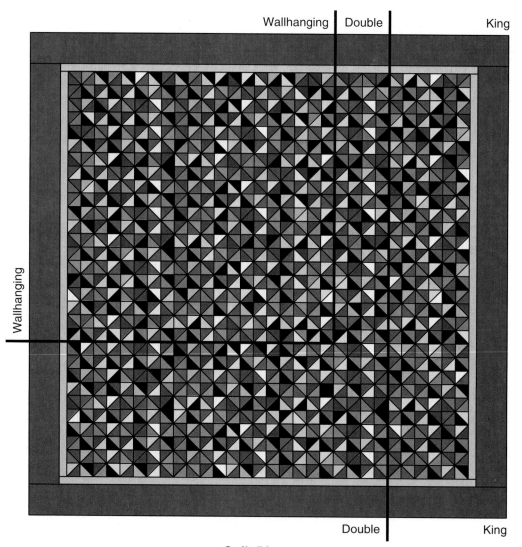

Quilt Diagram

Broken Dishes
Color Plan

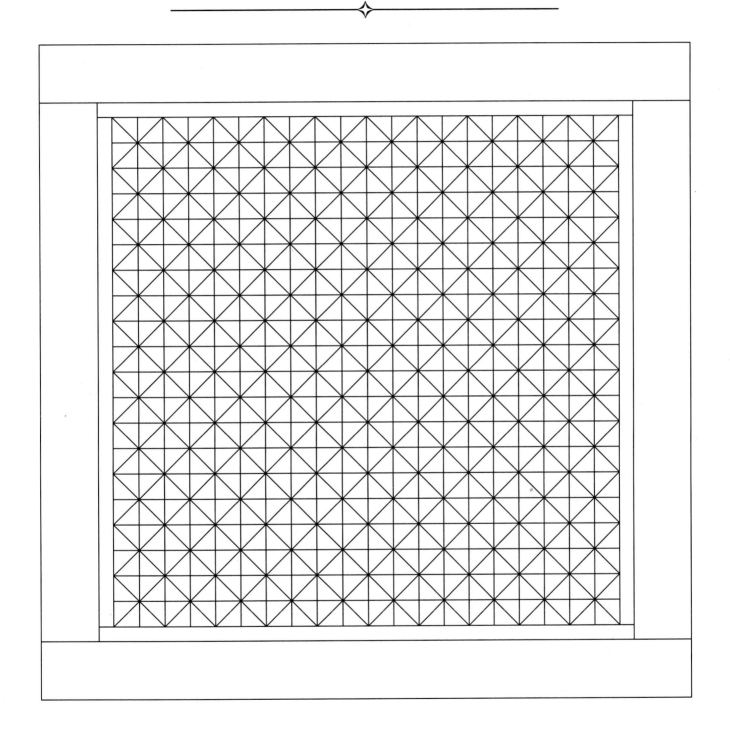

Photocopy this page and use it to experiment with color schemes for your quilt.

43

ROBBING PETER TO PAY PAUL

Skill Level: *Challenging*

Lively and vibrant, this quilt features a border formed by a skillful arrangement of color. Quiltmaker Becky Herdle of Rochester, New York, made this quilt over a two-year period while searching for an appropriate purple solid for the outer blocks. The quilt pattern is named Robbing Peter to Pay Paul because each assembled block "borrows" a portion from an adjacent block. The construction, however, isn't as difficult as it may seem since the blocks are actually square.

BEFORE YOU BEGIN

At first glance, this quilt appears to be pieced almost entirely with curved seams. While there are four curved seams within each block, the arcs are split lengthwise down the middle, allowing the blocks to be sewn together side by side with straight seams.

You will need to make templates from pattern pieces A and B on page 50. For information about making and using templates, see page 116.

This quilt has a unique border treatment. The blocks are assembled to form the quilt top, then the top is appliquéd onto the pre-assembled black borders. Read through the directions before beginning this project to become familiar with the various block types used.

CHOOSING FABRICS

The quiltmaker created the appearance of a border by using a consistent color scheme two blocks deep around the perimeter of the quilt. The inner portion of the quilt is sewn with a variety of solids in lighter values than those used around the edges.

To re-create the quilt shown, choose a black solid first, then select many clear, light solids in both warm and cool tones for the interior of the quilt. In this case, the quiltmaker used 12 different solids for the center area of the quilt top.

To help develop your own unique color scheme for the quilt, photocopy the **Color Plan** on page 51, and use crayons or colored pencils to experiment with different color arrangements.

CUTTING

All measurements include a ¼-inch seam allowance. Referring to the Cutting Chart, cut the re-

Quilt Sizes		
	Twin	Double (shown)
Finished Quilt Size	69" × 89"	79" × 89"
Finished Block Size	5"	5"
Number of Blocks	221	255

Materials		
	Twin	Double
Black	6¾ yards	7¾ yards
Assorted light solids	4¼ yards	5¼ yards
Purple	2¾ yards	3 yards
Pink	1⅔ yards	1⅞ yards
Turquoise	1⅛ yards	1¼ yards
Backing	5½ yards	5½ yards
Batting	75" × 95"	85" × 95"
Binding	¾ yard	¾ yard

NOTE: Yardages are based on 44/45-inch-wide fabrics that are at least 42 inches wide after preshrinking.

Cutting Chart

Fabric	Used For	Piece	Number to Cut	
			Twin	Double
Black	Background	A	162	183
	Arcs	B	156	200
Assorted light solids	Background	A	59	72
	Arcs	B	268	324
Purple	Arcs	B	260	280
Pink	Arcs	B	156	168
Turquoise	Arcs	B	104	112

Fabric	Used For	Strip Width	Number to Cut	
			Twin	Double
Black	Borders	4"	8	9

quired number of pieces for your quilt size. Pattern pieces A and B, on page 50, are used to cut all of the pieces for this quilt.

Note: Cut and piece one sample block before cutting all of the fabric for the quilt.

ASSEMBLING THE BLOCKS

Although all of the blocks are sewn in exactly the same manner, several color combinations were used to assemble the quilt shown on page 44. The **Block Diagram** illustrates the basic block types used in the quilt and gives you the total number of each block type required for your quilt size.

Types 1 and 2 are used two-deep along the top, bottom, and sides of the quilt. Types 3 and 4 are used in the outermost corners of the quilt. Type 5 is used to define the inside corners of the pieced "border." Types 6 and 7 are alternated in the center portion of the quilt. Type 8 is used to define the outer corner of the center portion of the quilt. Types 9 and 10 are used in the perimeter of the center portion of the quilt.

Step 1. Referring to **Diagram 1,** use a fine-point marker to mark the center of each curved side of a piece. Stack pieces by color.

Type 1
Make 48 for twin
Make 52 for double

Type 2
Make 48 for twin
Make 52 for double

Type 3
Make 2 for each quilt size

Type 4
Make 2 for each quilt size

Type 5
Make 4 for each quilt size

Type 6
Make 39 for twin
Make 50 for double

Type 7
Make 38 for twin
Make 49 for double

Type 8
Make 4 for each quilt size

Type 9
Make 16 for twin
Make 18 for double

Type 10
Make 20 for twin
Make 22 for double

Block Diagram

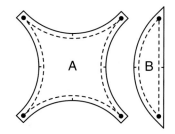

Diagram 1

Step 2. To make Type 1 blocks, gather one black A background, one turquoise B arc, two pink B arcs, and one purple B arc. With right sides together and the black A piece on top, match the center of the curved side of the turquoise arc with the center of one side of the black A piece, then pin at this point, as shown in **Diagram 2A.** Match the dots at the seam allowances and pin along the entire arc, as shown in **2B.** Sew the pinned pieces together. Press the seam toward the A piece.

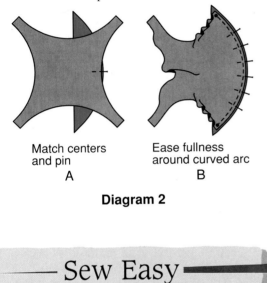

Match centers and pin
A

Ease fullness around curved arc
B

Diagram 2

— Sew Easy —

To reduce bulk in the seams before sewing the blocks together, trim a scant $1/8$ inch from the seam allowance near the block corners.

Step 3. Add the three remaining arcs in the same manner. Sew a purple arc directly across from the turquoise arc, and sew the two pink arcs in the remaining slots across from each other, as shown in the **Block Diagram.** Press seams toward the A piece. Assemble the total number of Type 1 blocks required for your quilt size. Stack the blocks together and label them.

Step 4. To make blocks 2 through 10, use one A background and four B arcs, referring to the **Block Diagram** for color placement. Press seams toward the A piece.

ASSEMBLING THE QUILT

Step 1. Use a design wall or other flat surface to lay out the completed blocks and remaining purple arcs around the outer edge, as shown in the **Assembly Diagrams.**

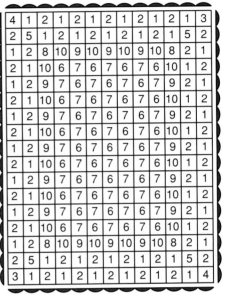

Twin

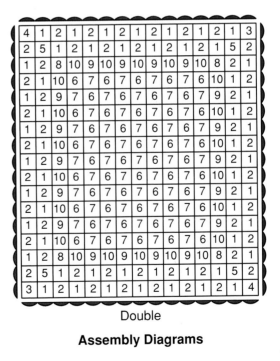

Double

Assembly Diagrams

Step 2. Sew the straight side of a purple arc to the straight side of each turquoise arc in the outermost blocks around the entire perimeter of the quilt, as shown in **Diagram 3.** Leave the seams unpressed until the rows are sewn together.

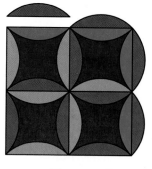

Diagram 3

Step 3. Sew the blocks in each horizontal row together. Press the seams in adjacent rows in opposite directions. Match the seams carefully, and sew the rows together. Press the quilt.

········· Sew Quick ········

If you made extra blocks, or if you kept your practice block, use it for a ready-made quilt label for the back of your quilt. A block with a light-colored center makes an ideal surface for recording the quilt's name, design and color inspiration, date of completion, and your signature.

MAKING THE OUTER BORDER

The outside edge of the quilt is centered and appliquéd to a preassembled border unit.

Step 1. To make the border unit for the twin-size quilt, piece together 4-inch-wide black strips, then cut two 67½-inch pieces for the top and bottom borders and two 91½-inch pieces for the side borders. For the double-size quilt, piece together 4-inch-wide black strips, then cut two 77½-inch pieces for the top and bottom borders and two 91½-inch pieces for the side borders.

Step 2. Beginning at any corner, sew a side border to a top or bottom border, as shown in **Diagram 4A,** placing the right sides together. Press the seam open, as shown in **4B.** Repeat for all corners to assemble the border, as shown in **4C.**

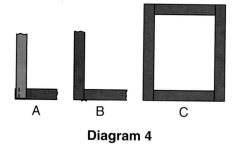

A   B   C

Diagram 4

APPLIQUÉING THE TOP TO THE BORDER

Step 1. Make a plastic template the size of a finished arc, represented by the dashed lines on template B. Trace the shape onto the nonwaxy side of freezer paper, and cut it out. Make a freezer paper template for each of the arcs around the outer edge of the quilt.

Step 2. Align a freezer paper arc, waxy side up, with the wrong side of an outer purple arc. The freezer paper should fit snugly against the inner seam allowance where the purple arc connects to the blue arc. Use a medium-hot iron to press the outer seam allowance of the arc onto the freezer paper, as shown in **Diagram 5.** Repeat, pressing a new freezer paper template onto each outer arc.

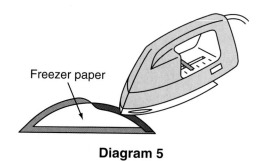

Freezer paper

Diagram 5

Step 3. Center and pin the quilt on the border. Two inches of black fabric should extend past the outer rings on all sides. Appliqué the quilt edges to the border and remove all freezer paper templates.

Step 4. Mark around a plate or other circular object to make a curve at each corner. Be sure the plate is in the same position for each corner so the curves will be the same size, as shown in **Diagram 6.** Trim the fabric outside the marked lines.

Diagram 6

QUILTING AND FINISHING

Step 1. Mark the quilt top for quilting. The quilt shown has cross-hatching in the centers of all of the background A pieces. All A and B pieces were outline quilted ¼ inch away from seam allowances. The black border area was not quilted.

Step 2. To make the backing for the twin-size quilt, cut the backing fabric in half crosswise, and trim the selvages. Cut two 18-inch-wide panels from one of the pieces, and sew a narrow panel to each side of the full-size piece, as shown in **Diagram 7** on page 50. Press the seams open.

Quilt Diagram

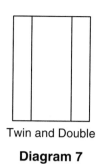

Twin and Double

Diagram 7

vages. Cut one piece in half lengthwise, and sew a narrow panel to each side of the full-width piece. Press the seams open.

Step 4. Layer the quilt top, batting, and backing, and baste the layers together. Quilt as desired.

Step 5. Use the remaining black fabric to make and attach double-fold bias binding, referring to page 121. To calculate the amount of binding needed for the quilt size you are making, add the length of the four sides of the quilt, plus 9 inches.

Step 3. For the double-size quilt, cut the backing fabric in half crosswise, and trim the sel-

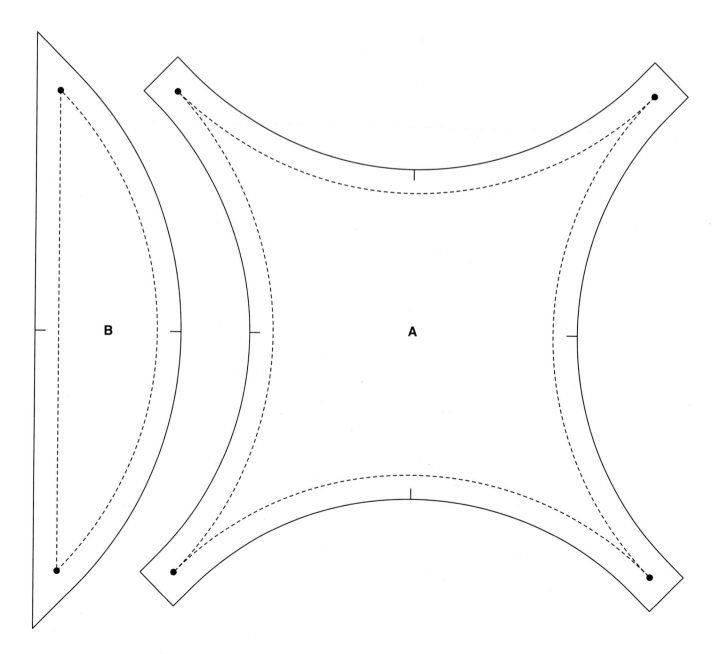

ROBBING PETER
TO PAY PAUL
Color Plan

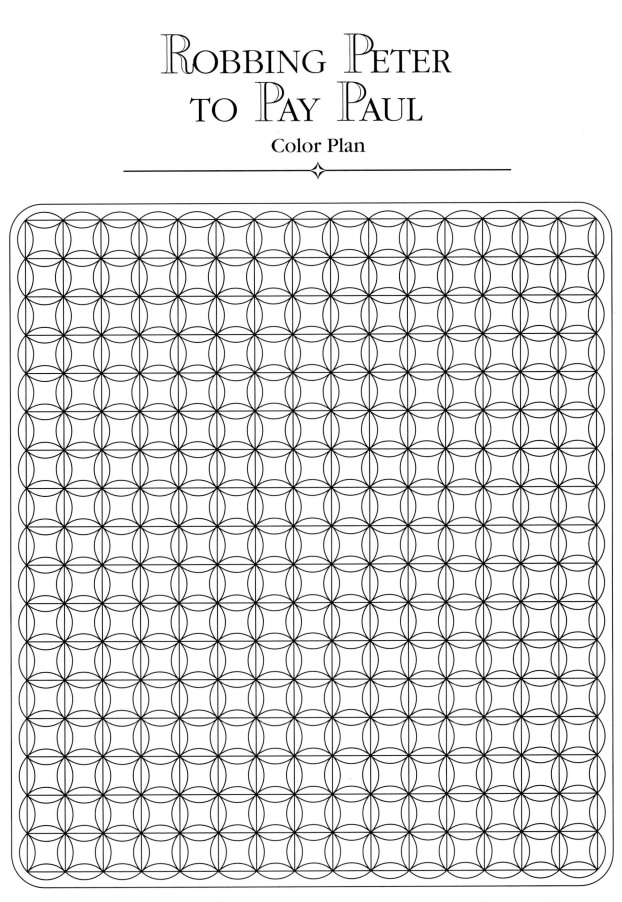

Photocopy this page and use it to experiment with color schemes for your quilt.

CHINESE COINS VARIATION
Skill Level: *Intermediate*

After admiring a similar Amish quilt, Karan Flanscha of Cedar Falls, Iowa, decided this Chinese Coins variation would be the perfect project for trying out her antique treadle sewing machine. She says she gained a greater appreciation for electric sewing machines with built-in lights and had finally mastered "pumping" the treadle by the time she finished piecing the top. Even though Karan's wallhanging was recently completed, it features colors and quilting patterns associated with antique Amish quilts.

BEFORE YOU BEGIN

This quilt is a variation of the Chinese Coins pattern, which itself is a variation of the Bars pattern described on page 23. Here, narrow bars of equilateral triangles are used to separate the bars of stacked "coins." The coins are easily assembled with a strip piecing technique; the triangles are alternated and sewn together to create a narrow bar. To eliminate the need for a triangle-shaped template, the triangles are rotary cut from a fabric strip.

CHOOSING FABRICS

Collect as many Amish-inspired colors as possible to re-create the scrappy effect of the quilt shown. Be sure to include light, medium, and dark fabrics. The yardages given in the materials chart are a guide and assume that you will choose equally from the three different values. For example, the total yardage required for the assorted colors in the wallhanging is 3 yards. Buy ⅛ yard of 24 different colors, 8 from each color value, to get the most impact. For the larger quilts, quarter-yard cuts of fabric will give you a wide variety of color choices.

In the quilt on the opposite page, the inner and outer borders are sewn from fabrics of the same value. Although the colors themselves are entirely different, the two fabrics blend together when viewed from a distance.

To help develop your own unique color scheme for the quilt, photocopy the **Color Plan** on page 59, and use crayons or colored pencils to experiment with different color arrangements.

Quilt Sizes

	Wallhanging (shown)	Twin	Double
Finished Quilt Size	46¾" × 35"	69¾" × 97"	81¼" × 97"
Number of Bars			
Coins	7	11	13
Triangle	6	10	12

Materials

	Wallhanging	Twin	Double
Assorted lights	1 yard	2¾ yards	3 yards
Assorted mediums	1 yard	2¾ yards	3 yards
Assorted darks	1 yard	2¾ yards	3 yards
Forest green	⅜ yard	¾ yard	⅞ yard
Orchid	¼ yard	½ yard	½ yard
Backing	1⅝ yards	5⅞ yards	7⅝ yards
Batting	52" × 41"	76" × 103"	87" × 103"
Binding	⅜ yard	¾ yard	¾ yard

NOTE: Yardages are based on 44/45-inch-wide fabrics that are at least 42 inches wide after preshrinking.

Cutting Chart

Fabric	Used For	Strip Width	Number to Cut		
			Wallhanging	Twin	Double
Assorted lights, mediums, and darks	Equilateral triangles	2¾"	12*	32	38
	Coin bars	1"–3½"	See "Cutting" below		
Forest green	Outer border	3"	4	8	9
Orchid	Inner border	2"	4	8	8

*Cut 21-inch-long strips, instead of 42-inch-long strips, to provide more color variety.

CUTTING

All measurements include ¼-inch seam allowances. Referring to the Cutting Chart, cut the required number of strips in the width needed. Cut all strips across the fabric width.

Equilateral triangles are quick-cut from strips of fabric. Triangles used at the ends of bars are cut from rectangles. Stacks of coins are sewn together using quick-piecing techniques, then trimmed to the exact width and length required before the quilt top is assembled.

For the coin bars, cut at least two strips from each of the assorted light, medium, and dark fabrics, varying the strip widths between 1 and 3½ inches wide. When cutting strips, keep in mind that ½ inch of the total width of each strip will be lost in seam allowances. Cut at least three strips from each fabric for the twin size and at least four strips for the double size. Cut each strip into three 14-inch-long pieces.

For the end triangles, cut six 3¼ × 1¾-inch rectangles from various colors for the wallhanging. Cut 10 rectangles for the twin-size and 12 rectangles for the double-size quilt.

ASSEMBLING THE COIN BARS

To obtain the correct length for the coin bars, you will make strip sets 10 and 20 inches wide, then use a combination of both sizes to make the coin bars.

Step 1. Match the edges and sew the assorted color straight-of-grain strips together lengthwise to form the coin bars, as shown in **Diagram 1**. Vary the strip width and color to create a pleasing mixture. Continue sewing strips together until your strip set is approximately 20 inches wide.

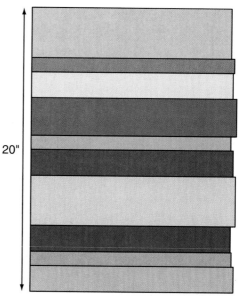

Diagram 1

Step 2. Press all of the seams in one direction. Using a rotary cutter and ruler, square up one side of the pressed set, then cut three 4¼-inch-wide segments from it to form the coin bar segments, as shown in **Diagram 2**.

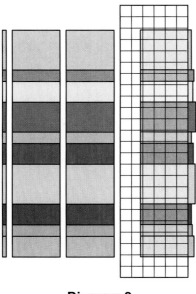

Diagram 2

Step 3. Assemble additional coin bar segments in the same manner as in Steps 1 and 2, making strip sets as follows: For the wallhanging, make seven 10- and seven 20-inch-wide segments. For the twin size, make eleven 10- and forty-four 20-inch-wide segments. For the double size, make thirteen 10- and fifty-two 20-inch-wide segments.

Step 4. For the wallhanging, sew one 10- and one 20-inch segment together along the 4$\frac{1}{4}$-inch edges to create a coin bar (see **Diagram 3**). Repeat to make a total of seven coin bars. Trim each bar to 27 inches. Repeat for the twin and double size, sewing one 10-inch and four 20-inch segments together to create a coin bar. Make 11 coin bars for the twin size and 13 for the double size. Trim the coin bars for both sizes to 89 inches.

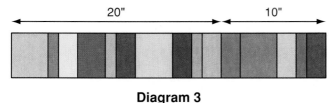

Diagram 3

ASSEMBLING THE TRIANGLE BARS

Step 1. Align the 60-degree angle line on your ruler with the bottom left edge of one equilateral

triangle strip, and make the cut illustrated in **Diagram 4**.

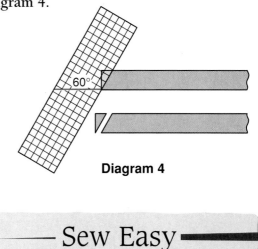

Diagram 4

Sew Easy

If your ruler is slipping when you cut small pieces like the 60-degree triangles, glue small pieces of fine-grit sandpaper to the underside of the ruler.

Step 2. Mark the strip in 3$\frac{1}{8}$-inch increments, beginning at the lower left edge of the strip, as shown in **Diagram 5**. Cut the triangles as shown, rotating your ruler between cuts so that the 60-degree line is always aligned with either the top or bottom edge of the strip. Cut 132 triangles for the wallhanging, 760 for the twin, and 912 for the double. Sort the triangles by color value.

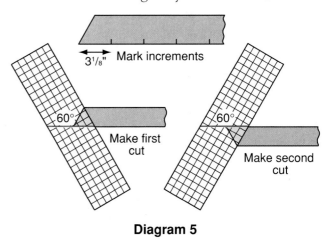

Diagram 5

Step 3. End triangles, or half-equilateral triangles, are used at the top and bottom of the triangle bars. To make an end triangle, cut each 1¾ × 3¼-inch rectangle in half diagonally, as shown in **Diagram 6A**. Keeping the cut rectangles together as a unit, divide the pile in half. Label one half "odd." Flip the remaining half of the cut rectangles over so the cut is in the opposite direction and label them "even."

Note: If you are using a print fabric or a solid fabric that isn't the same color on both sides, cut one half of the rectangles diagonally in one direction, labeling them "odd"; cut the other half of the rectangles in half diagonally in the other direction, labeling them "even," as shown in **Diagram 6B**. Cut a total of 12 end triangles for the wallhanging, 20 for the twin size, and 24 for the double size, making half "odd" triangles and half "even" triangles.

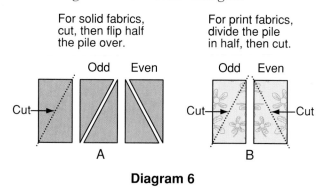

Diagram 6

Step 4. Sew the end triangles and equilateral triangles into bars, alternating fabrics for good contrast. For the wallhanging, sew 22 equilateral triangles together, then add one "odd" end triangle to each end, as shown in **Diagram 7A**. Make six triangle bars, three of which should have "odd" end triangles and three of which should have "even" end triangles, as shown in **7B**. Once the bars are assembled, stack and label them "odd" or "even."

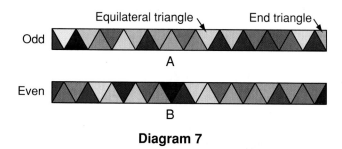

Diagram 7

Both the twin- and double-size quilts have 76 equilateral triangles in each triangle bar. Make 10 triangle bars for the twin size and 12 for the double size. Sew "odd" end triangles to half of the bars and "even" end triangles to the other half. Stack and label the triangle bars "odd" or "even."

ASSEMBLING THE QUILT TOP

Step 1. Arrange the coin bars and the triangle bars into rows side by side, beginning and ending with a coin bar and alternating "odd" and "even" triangle bars. Refer to the **Wallhanging Assembly Diagram** or the **Twin- and Double-Size Assembly Diagram**. Make sure the coin bars are at least as long as the triangle bars. If not, sew an additional 4¼-inch-wide strip of fabric to the top or bottom to increase the length.

Step 2. Pin the bars together lengthwise, matching the top edges. Be sure the equilateral triangle bases are directly across from each other. Sew the seams, then press them toward the coin bars. Trim the coin bars flush with the triangle bars.

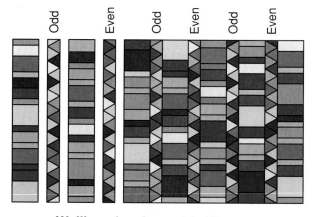

Wallhanging Assembly Diagram

ATTACHING THE BORDERS

Step 1. Attach the top and bottom borders first, referring to the **Wallhanging Diagram** or the **Twin-Size Quilt Diagram**. Measure the width of the quilt top, taking the measurement through the horizontal center of the quilt. Sew the orchid strips together to make two borders this exact length.

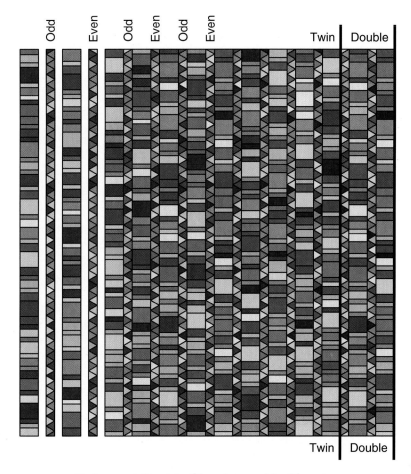

Odd Even Odd Even Odd Even   Twin | Double

Twin | Double

Twin- and Double-Size Assembly Diagram

Step 2. Fold one of the strips in half crosswise and crease. Unfold it and position it right side down along the top of the quilt, with the crease at the vertical midpoint. Pin at the midpoint and ends first, then along the length of the entire edge, easing in fullness as necessary. Sew the border to the quilt. Repeat for the bottom border. Press seams toward the borders.

Step 3. Measure the length of the quilt, taking the measurement through the vertical center of the quilt and including the top and bottom borders. Using the orchid strips, piece two border strips this exact length and sew these to the sides of the quilt, in the same manner as in Step 2. Press.

Step 4. In the same manner, prepare and add the outer borders to the quilt, using the 3-inch forest green strips. Attach the top and bottom borders first, and be sure to include the borders when measuring the length of the quilt for the side borders.

QUILTING AND FINISHING

Step 1. Mark the quilt top for quilting. The quilt shown features a thick cable design for the middle and two outer coin bars, a pumpkin seed motif and a simple flower vine for the remaining coin bars, and a leaf design for the triangle bars. The borders were treated as a single unit and feature a stylized swirl that spans the width of both.

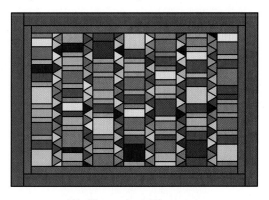

Wallhanging Diagram

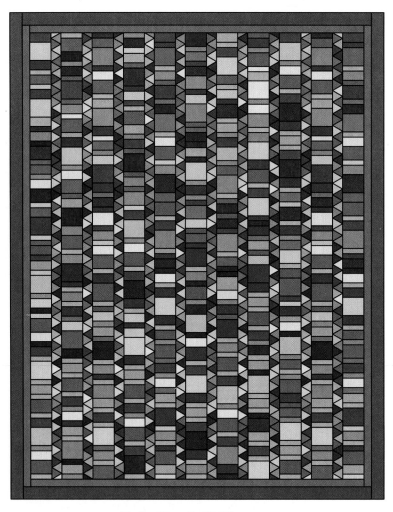

Twin-Size Quilt Diagram

Step 2. If you are making the wallhanging, the backing does not have to be pieced, as shown in **Diagram 8.** For the twin-size quilt, cut the backing fabric crosswise into two equal pieces and trim the selvages. Cut two 18-inch-wide segments from one piece. Sew a narrow segment to each side of the full-width piece, as shown in the diagram. Press the seams open.

Step 3. For the double-size quilt, cut the backing fabric crosswise into three equal pieces, and trim the selvages. Cut 31-inch-wide segments from two of the pieces, then sew one of the narrow segments to each side of the full-width piece as shown in the diagram. Press the seams open.

Step 4. Layer the quilt top, batting, and backing, and baste the layers together. Quilt as desired.

Step 5. Referring to the directions on page 121, make and attach double-fold binding. To calculate the amount of binding needed for the quilt size you are making, add the length of the four sides of the quilt, plus 9 inches.

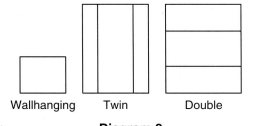

Wallhanging   Twin   Double

Diagram 8

CHINESE COINS VARIATION
Color Plan

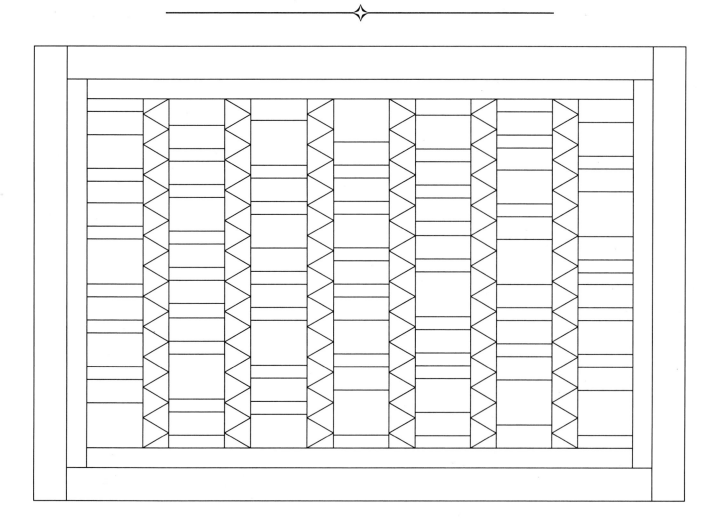

Photocopy this page and use it to experiment with color schemes for your quilt.

LOG CABIN

Skill Level: *Intermediate*

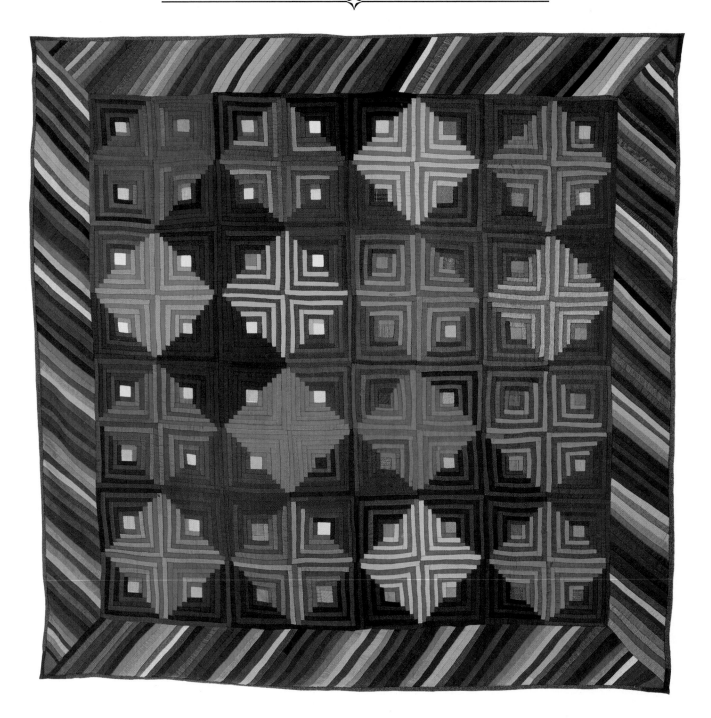

his dramatic Log Cabin quilt was made in the early 1880s by
Paulina "Polly" Hostetler, prior to her marriage to David Miller.
Polly was born on January 15, 1863, and lived most of her life in
Holmes County, Ohio. Family members recall that this quilt was never
used; it was kept in a drawer and taken out and enjoyed from time to
time. It is currently cared for by Polly's maternal grandson, Abner
Schlabach of Perkasie, Pennsylvania.

BEFORE YOU BEGIN

The blocks and borders in this quilt are pieced on a foundation, since that technique makes working with narrow strips of fabric a breeze. It takes a little bit of practice to learn to position the fabric strips correctly, but you'll be a pro after sewing a block or two. If this technique is new to you, be sure to read through the instructions before beginning the project.

CHOOSING FABRICS

While this quilt was sewn from an assortment of wools and rayons, we recommend 100 percent cotton solids, because they are durable and easy to work with.

To make this quilt, choose a selection of fabrics from four color values: very dark, dark, medium bright, and light. Choose subdued tones for your darks, and rich, vibrant colors for your medium brights and lights.

One half of each block is sewn with fabrics from the two darkest values and the other half is sewn from the medium bright and light values, with the visual division along the diagonal center of the block. The quiltmaker used sev-

eral different fabrics for each color value in her quilt, but yours can be sewn quite successfully with fewer variations.

You will make two versions of the Log Cabin block because the two blocks are built in different directions and their color values vary. The diamonds in the final

design are created when the lighter portions of four blocks are positioned together. The dark and light diamonds become more obvious with increasing contrast between the two block halves.

To help develop your own unique color scheme for the quilt, photocopy the **Color Plan**

Quilt Sizes			
	Wallhanging (shown)	Double	King
Finished Quilt Size	67½" × 67½"	81½" × 95½"	109½" × 109½"
Finished Block Size	7"	7"	7"
Number of Blocks	64	120	196

Materials			
	Wallhanging	Double	King
Assorted lights	3 yards	5 yards	7⅛ yards
Assorted darks	2⅞ yards	4½ yards	7⅛ yards
Assorted very darks	2⅝ yards	4¼ yards	6⅛ yards
Assorted medium brights	2½ yards	4 yards	5⅞ yards
Backing	4¼ yards	5⅞ yards	10 yards
Batting	74" × 74"	88" × 102"	116" × 116"
Binding	⅝ yard	¾ yard	⅞ yard

NOTE: *Yardages are based on 44/45-inch-wide fabrics that are at least 42 inches wide after preshrinking.*

Cutting Chart

Fabric	Used For	Strip Width	Number to Cut		
			Wallhanging	Double	King
Assorted lights	Blocks and borders	1¼"	61	120	183
	Block centers	1½"	3	5	7
Assorted darks	Blocks and borders	1¼"	76	107	193
Assorted very darks	Blocks and borders	1¼"	67	110	165
Assorted medium brights	Blocks and borders	1¼"	62	102	153

on page 69, and use crayons or colored pencils to experiment with different color arrangements.

CUTTING

The finished width of the logs in this quilt is ½ inch. For foundation piecing, use strips a little wider than those required for traditional piecing, since wider strips give you more flexibility as you position them on the back of the foundation. The Cutting Chart calls for strips that are wider than necessary. However, since it will only take a practice block or two for you to become comfortable with the technique, you may not want to cut extra-wide strips for the entire quilt. Cut just enough to construct one or two blocks, then re-evaluate the strip width, reducing it when you feel comfortable doing so. Never cut the strips narrower than the finished width plus a ¼-inch seam allowance (1 inch wide) on each side.

The striped border is foundation pieced from the same strips used for the blocks. As you piece the blocks, set aside extra strips that are at least 10 inches long for use in the border.

From the 1½-inch-wide assorted light strips, cut 1½-inch squares for the block centers. You will need 64 squares for the wallhanging, 120 squares for the bed topper, and 196 squares for the king-size quilt.

Note: Cut and piece one sample block on a foundation before cutting all of the fabric for the quilt.

MAKING THE FOUNDATIONS

Use the **Block Pattern** on page 68 to prepare a separate paper foundation for each quilt block; photocopy or trace the block to prepare the foundations. For the wallhanging, make foundations for 32 A and 32 B blocks. For the bed topper, make foundations for 60 A and 60 B blocks. For the king size, make foundations for 98 A and 98

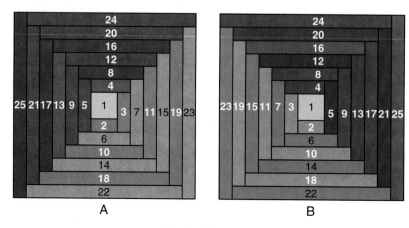

A   B

Block Diagram

B blocks. Make sure the marked lines are visible from the back side when you hold the foundation up to the light. Use the **Block Diagram** and the **Block Pattern** as color guides and references for piecing order. The light half of the A blocks starts with a medium bright for logs 2 and 3, then alternates outward, ending with a light. The dark half of the A blocks starts with a dark for logs 4 and 5, then alternates outward, ending with a very dark. The light half of the B blocks starts with a light for logs 2 and 3, then alternates outward, ending with a medium bright. The dark half of the B blocks starts with a very dark for logs 4 and 5, then alternates outward, ending with a dark. Transfer value designations marked on each log to the foundations.

PIECING THE BLOCKS

Step 1. Strips are positioned on the back or un-marked side of the foundation. Logs are added in numerical order, and all sewing takes place on the front side, directly on the drawn lines. All lines on the foundation, except the one around the outer perimeter, are seam lines. To begin, place a 1½-inch center square right side up on the back side of your foundation, centering it over the lines surrounding the area for log 1, as shown in **Diagram 1.** Use tape, a dab of glue stick, or a pin to hold the fabric in place. This is the only piece that will be positioned right side up; all others will be positioned right side down for sewing.

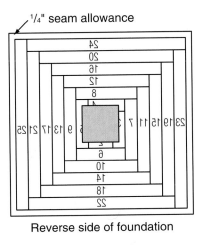

Reverse side of foundation

Diagram 1

Step 2. Hold the foundation up to the light with the back side away from you. You should be able to see the shadow of log 1. Does the shadow overlap all lines drawn for log 1? Is the overlap sufficient to create a stable seam allowance? If not, reposition the piece and check it again.

Step 3. Find the strip of fabric set aside for log 2 and position it on the back side of your foundation, right side down. Align the strip along the left and lower edges of log 1, as shown in **Diagram 2A.** The strip will entirely cover log 1. Keep the strip's grain-line parallel to the seam lines. Holding the strip in place, flip the foundation over to its front side. Making 12–14 stitches per inch, sew on the line separating log 1 from log 2, beginning and ending the stitching approximately ⅛ inch on either side of the line, as shown in **2B.**

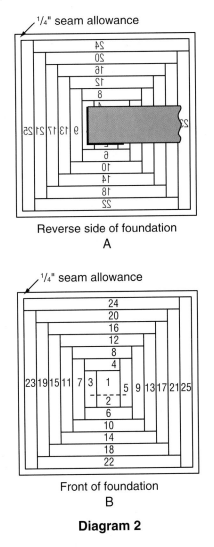

Reverse side of foundation
A

Front of foundation
B

Diagram 2

Step 4. Flip again to the back side of your foundation. Trim away the excess fabric from log 2 approximately ⅛ inch past the end of the seam line, as shown in **Diagram 3A.** If necessary, trim away excess fabric from the seam allowance you've created. If you used tape to secure the first piece, remove it now. Flip log 2 into a right-side-up position, finger pressing it firmly into place. The back side of your foundation should now resemble **3B.**

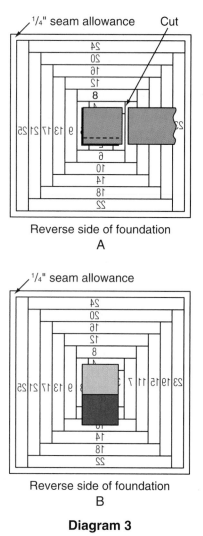

Reverse side of foundation
A

Reverse side of foundation
B

Diagram 3

Step 5. Hold the foundation up to the light with the back side away from you. You will now be able to see the shadow created by the fabric for log 2. Its raw edges should overlap all unsewn seam lines for log 2. This ensures that there will be sufficient seam allowance on all sides when you add the adjacent logs.

Step 6. Log 3 is added in exactly the same way as log 2. Position the strip of fabric right side down on the back of the foundation, aligning its top with log 1 and its left edges with the left edges of logs 1 and 2, as shown in **Diagram 4A.** The strip will completely cover the sewn pieces.

Flip the foundation over, and sew on the vertical line separating log 3 from logs 1 and 2, beginning and ending approximately ⅛ inch on either side of the line. Remove the foundation from the machine. Trim the excess tail and seam allowance from log 3. Flip log 3 into position right side up, finger pressing it into place. The reverse side of your foundation should now resemble **4B.**

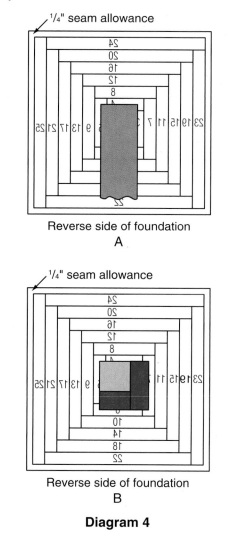

Reverse side of foundation
A

Reverse side of foundation
B

Diagram 4

Step 7. All remaining logs are added in exactly the same manner, working around the center in numerical order and following the color guidelines on the **Block Pattern.** You'll quickly develop a rhythm of placing a log, sewing a seam, trimming back, flipping the log upright, and checking its position. Each new seam you sew acts as a stabilizer for those it intersects with in the block.

——— Sew Easy ———

Notice that the back side of your foundation, where the fabric is sewn, is a mirror image of the drawn lines on the front. This can sometimes make color placement confusing. To help you keep track of color and value placement as you add logs to the foundation, jot the color name next to the numerical designation on the front of the foundation. Or, use colored pencils to color in the logs and give you an easy identifier.

Step 8. As you add the final four logs (numbers 22 through 25), make sure their outer edges extend slightly past the drawn seam allowance. After sewing log 25, press the entire block lightly. Align your plastic ruler with an *outer* line of the seam allowance, and cut directly on the line with your rotary cutter. Repeat for the remaining outer lines. Leave removable foundations in place until your quilt top is assembled to help stabilize the blocks and the seams.

Step 9. Repeat Steps 1 through 8, making three more identical color blocks, as shown in **Diagram 5A,** to make a total of 2 A blocks and 2 B blocks. Once the rows of the quilt are sewn together, the four-block cluster will create a diamond-shape pattern, as shown in **5B.** The quilt shown in the photograph on page 60 has the lighter portions of each four-block cluster together, creating a diamond shape. Continue making identical color, four-block clusters until you have assembled the total number of blocks required for the quilt size you're making.

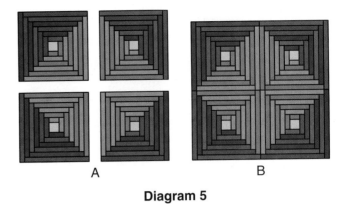

Diagram 5

ASSEMBLING THE QUILT TOP

Step 1. Referring to the **Assembly Diagram,** lay out the blocks in rows. Be sure to match lighter halves of blocks when positioning each block. The quilt shown is the wallhanging. For the double, you'll have 12 horizontal rows of 10 blocks each. For the king, you'll have 14 horizontal rows of 14 blocks each.

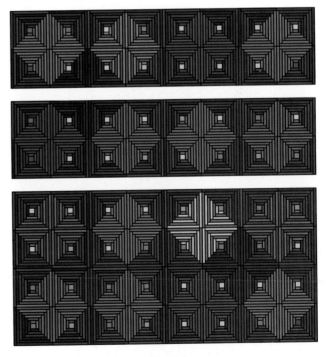

Assembly Diagram

Step 2. Sew the blocks together into horizontal rows. Press seams in adjoining rows in opposite directions, then sew the rows together, matching seams carefully. Press the quilt.

ASSEMBLING THE BORDERS

Step 1. Measure the quilt vertically through its center and add 16 inches to the measurement. That total is the length you must make each side border. Measure the quilt horizontally through its center and add 16 inches. That total is the length you must make the top and bottom borders.

Step 2. The borders are foundation pieced using 1¼-inch-wide strips of the same fabrics used in the blocks. Long border foundation strips can be made with accordion-like, pin-fed computer paper, or regular paper taped together end to end. Cut the paper 7 inches wide down the length of the foundation.

Step 3. Use your rotary ruler to draw a straight line just inside the lengthwise edge of the foundation. Draw another line 6 inches to the right of the first, as shown in **Diagram 6A**. The side seam allowances are included in the 6-inch measurement.

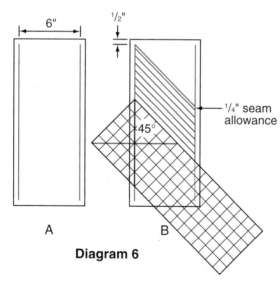

Diagram 6

Beginning approximately ½ inch from the top left corner of the foundation, use the 45-degree markings on your ruler to connect the straight lines with a series of 45-degree lines, ½ inch apart, as shown in **6B**. Stop drawing lines approximately ½ inch away from the lower right corner of the column. Draw a 45-degree line ¼ inch away from the top line for a seam allowance, as shown in the diagram; repeat below the bottom line.

Step 4. Sew fabric strips approximately 10 inches long to the foundation in the same manner as you did for the log cabin blocks. Place your first strip right side up on the back side of the foundation at one end of the marked column. Add more strips by positioning them right side down and sewing on the marked line on the front. Keep in mind that when flipped into a right side up position, the ends must cover all drawn lines of the foundation, as shown in **Diagram 7A**. Sew a seam through all layers, parallel to and approximately ⅛ inch inside each side seam allowance, as shown in **7B**.

Step 5. Trim all four outer lines of the column. Repeat Steps 2 through 4 until you have four borders of the lengths previously calculated. Sew the individual columns together for each border.

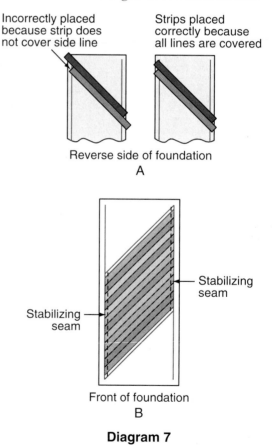

Diagram 7

Step 6. Referring to the **Quilt Diagram**, sew the borders to the quilt, mitering the corners according to the instructions on page 119.

Step 7. Tear away all removable foundations.

QUILTING AND FINISHING

Step 1. The quilt shown was not quilted. However, straight in-the-ditch quilting would be a good choice because of the number of seams.

Step 2. To make the backing for the wallhanging, cut the backing fabric into two equal lengths, and trim the selvages. Cut one piece in half lengthwise, and sew a narrow panel to each side of the full-width piece, as shown in **Diagram 8**. Press the seams open. For the double, cut the backing fabric into two equal lengths and trim the selvages. Sew the pieces together lengthwise, as shown in the diagram. Press the seams open. For the king-size quilt, cut the backing fabric into three equal lengths, and trim the selvages. Sew the three pieces together lengthwise, as shown in the diagram. Press the seams open.

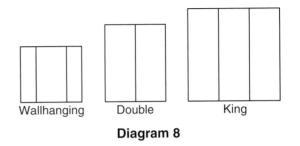

Diagram 8

Step 3. Layer the quilt top, batting, and backing, and baste the layers together. Quilt as desired.

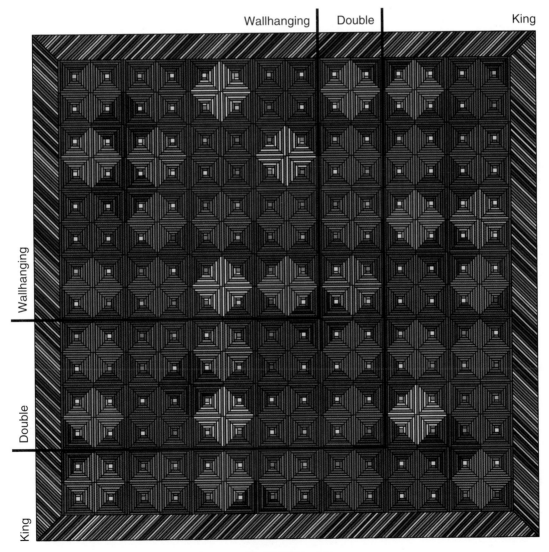

Quilt Diagram

Step 4. Referring to the directions on page 121 make and attach double-fold binding to finish at a width of 1 inch. To calculate the amount of binding needed for the quilt size you are making, add the length of the four sides of the quilt, plus 9 inches.

Key: Trace this foundation pattern for the A blocks, and use the colors indicated in black to make the blocks. The side with the traced lines is the front (or sewing side) of the foundation. For the B blocks, trace this foundation pattern onto tracing paper. This is the reverse (or fabric side) of the foundation. Turn the paper over, retrace the lines, and use the colors indicated in red to make the blocks. This is the front (or sewing side) of the foundation.

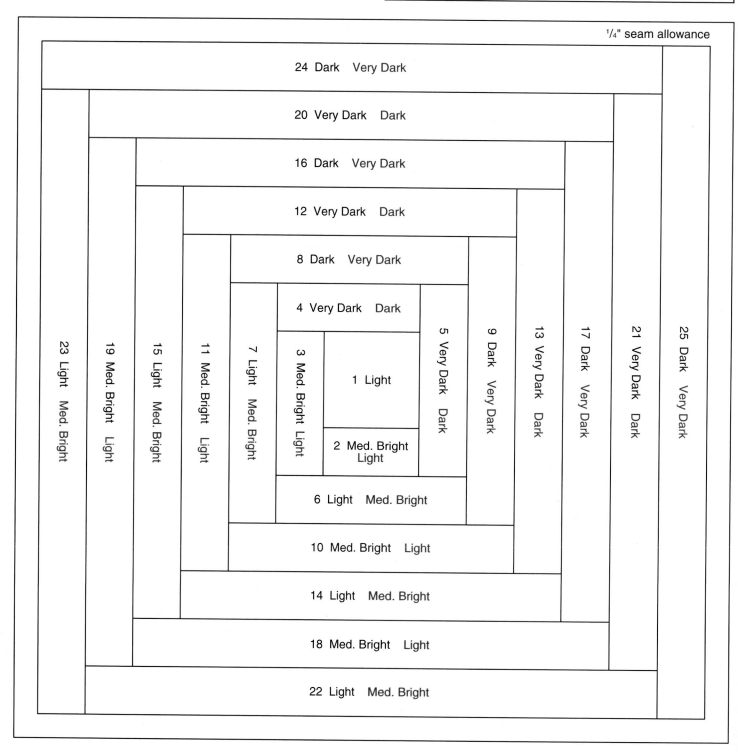

¼" seam allowance

Block Pattern

LOG CABIN
Color Plan

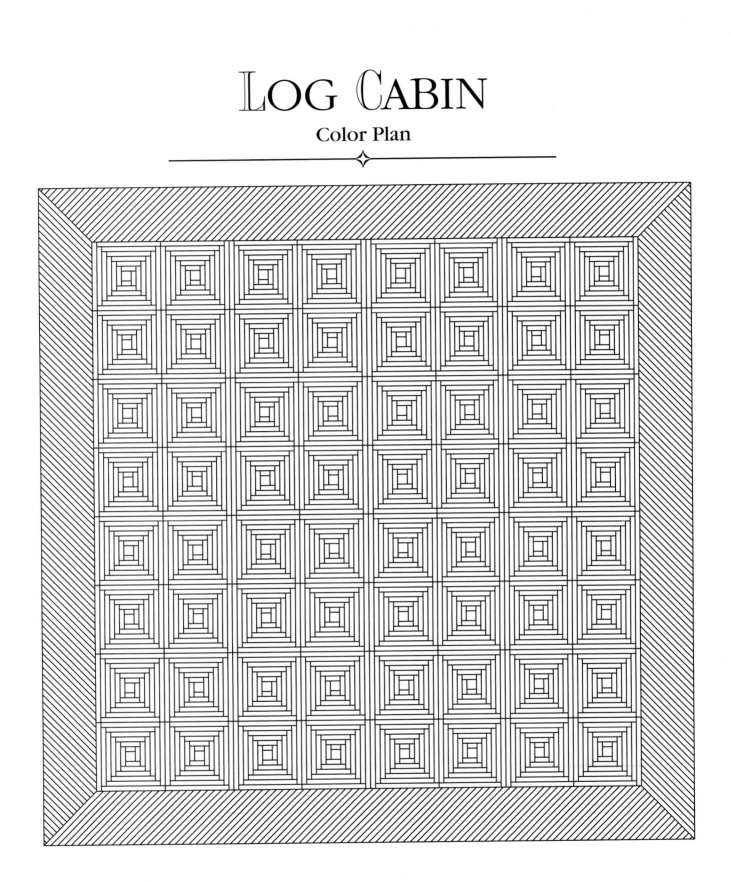

Photocopy this page and use it to experiment with color schemes for your quilt.

69

DOUBLE NINE PATCH

Skill Level: *Intermediate*

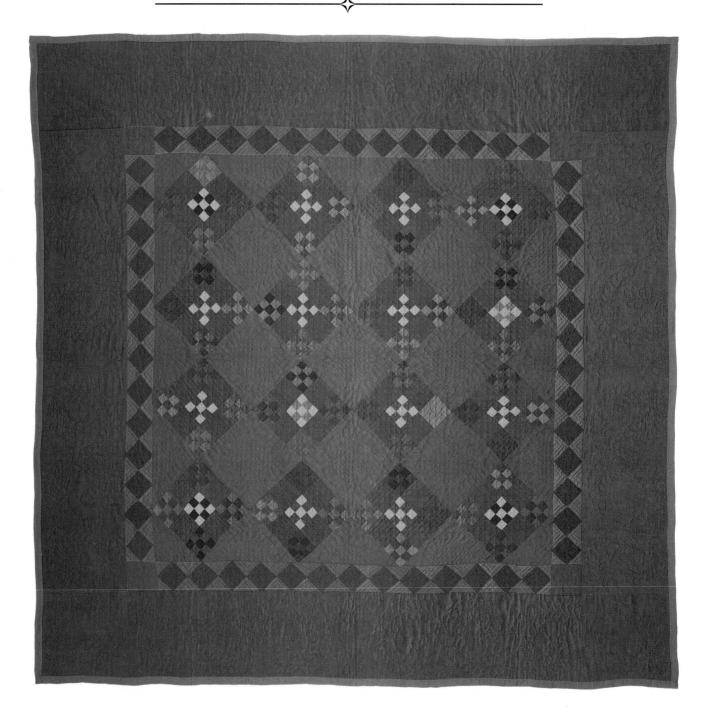

*T*his bright multiple-patch quilt was made in Lancaster County, Pennsylvania, in the 1930s. It is now part of a quilt collection owned by Douglas Tompkins of Puerto Montt, Chile. Young Amish girls often made a Double Nine Patch as their first piecing project. The straight lines and simple shapes are good practice for someone just learning to quilt, but the number of patches and the color combinations make it fun for someone with patchwork experience.

BEFORE YOU BEGIN

The instructions for this quilt are written based on using a quick-piecing method for making Nine Patch blocks. Strips of fabric are sewn together into strip sets. The strip sets are then cut apart and sewn into blocks.

Each Double Nine Patch block in this quilt is composed of five 3-inch Nine Patch blocks and four 3-inch setting squares. The Double Nine Patch blocks are set on point in the quilt, with setting squares and triangles used to separate them. The inner border is pieced with squares set on point.

CHOOSING FABRICS

Each Nine Patch block in this quilt is sewn with two solid fabrics. Although there should be contrast between the two fabrics, this quilt uses scraps of fabrics in many colors and values. For instance, the Nine Patch blocks used at the centers of each Double Nine Patch block stand out because of the high contrast between the two fabrics. The quiltmaker chose to use the same pink for the center of each Nine Patch block, but you can use an assortment of colors. To simplify cutting and piecing the Nine Patch blocks, directions are given as though each Double Nine Patch block has darker blocks in the four corners and a lighter block in the center, even though

Quilt Sizes

	Bed Topper (shown)	King
Finished Quilt Size	85" × 85"	110½" × 110½"
Finished Block Size		
Double Nine Patch	9"	9"
Nine Patch	3"	3"
Number of Blocks		
Double Nine Patch	16	36
Corner Nine Patch	64	144
Center Nine Patch	16	36

Materials

	Bed Topper	King
Red	2⅞ yards	3⅞ yards
Green	2⅛ yards	3¼ yards
Assorted darks	1⅜ yards	1⅝ yards
Assorted lights	1⅜ yards	1⅞ yards
Beige	⅞ yard	1 yard
Gray	¾ yard	1¼ yards
Purple	½ yard	¾ yard
Backing	7¾ yards	10 yards
Batting	91" × 91"	117" × 117"
Binding	1½ yards	1⅝ yards

NOTE: *Yardages are based on 44/45-inch-wide fabrics that are at least 42 inches wide after preshrinking.*

Cutting Chart

Fabric	Used For	Strip Width	Number to Cut Bed Topper	King
Red	Setting squares	9½"	3	7
	Side setting triangles	14"	1	2
	Corner triangles	7¼"	1	1
	Inner border corners	4¾"	1	1
	Outer border corners	12¼"	2	2
Green	Outer border	12¼"	6	9
Assorted darks	Strip sets	1½"	15	20
Assorted lights	Strip sets	1½"	30	40
Beige	Inner border side setting triangles	5½"	4	5
	Inner border setting corners	3"	1	1
Gray	Setting squares	3½"	6	12
Purple	Inner border squares	3½"	4	6

the quilt shown uses both dark and light blocks in the corners.

Carefully consider the fabric you choose for the setting squares. A neutral gray was used in the quilt shown, and it recedes into the background, allowing the bright colors used in the Nine Patch blocks to be the focal point.

The light and dark yardages shown are generous estimates of the total yardage used in the quilt. Since small amounts of many fabrics are a key ingredient for a successful scrap-look quilt, you will likely begin with more yardage than you need to allow for a wider variety of colors in the Nine Patch blocks. For the greatest assortment of colors, purchase fabric in ⅛-yard cuts.

To help develop your own unique color scheme, photocopy the **Color Plan** on page 77, and use crayons or colored pencils to experiment with different color arrangements.

CUTTING

All measurements include ¼-inch seam allowances. Referring to the Cutting Chart, cut the required number of strips in the width needed.

Cut all strips across the fabric width.

• For the setting squares, cut the 9½-inch red strips into 9½-inch squares.

• For the side setting triangles, cut the 14-inch red strips into 14-inch squares. Cut each square in half twice diagonally, as shown in **Diagram 1A.**

• For the corner triangles, cut the 7¼-inch red strip into 7¼-inch squares. Cut each square in half diagonally, as shown in **1B.**

• For the inner border corners, cut the 4¾-inch red strip into 4¾-inch squares.

• For the outer border corners, cut the 12¼-inch red strips into 12¼-inch squares.

• For the inner border side setting triangles, cut the 5½-inch beige strips into 5½-inch squares. Cut each square in half twice diagonally.

• For the inner border setting corners, cut the 3-inch beige strip into 3-inch squares. Cut each square in half diagonally.

• For the setting squares, cut the 3½-inch gray strips into 3½-inch squares.

• For the inner border squares, cut the 3½-inch purple strips into 3½-inch squares.

Note: Cut and piece one sample block before cutting all of the fabric for the quilt.

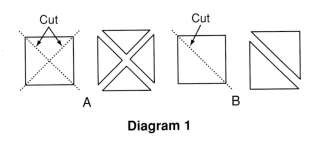

Diagram 1

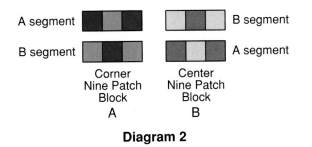

Diagram 2

PIECING THE NINE PATCH BLOCKS

Each Double Nine Patch block is made up of five Nine Patch blocks (four corner Nine Patch blocks and one center Nine Patch block) and four setting squares, as shown in the **Block Diagram.** Each corner Nine Patch block is strip-pieced with a dark fabric as the main fabric and a light fabric as the accent. The center Nine Patch blocks are just the opposite—the light fabric is the main fabric and the dark fabric is the accent.

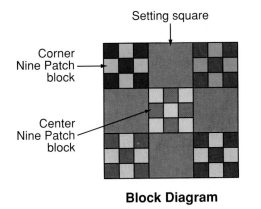

Block Diagram

Step 1. Each Nine Patch block requires two different segment variations. Refer to **Diagram 2A** for positioning dark and light fabrics for the corner Nine Patch block. Refer to **2B** for positioning dark and light fabrics for the center Nine Patch block. There are two A segments and one B segment in each corner Nine Patch block and one A segment and two B segments in each center Nine Patch block. The directions given here will allow you to piece five blocks at one time from the same two fabrics. Using short strips, you can duplicate the scrappiness of the quilt shown while still taking advantage of the accuracy and speed of quick-piecing methods.

Step 2. Separate the strips into light and dark piles. Select a dark strip and a light strip from the piles. From the dark strip, cut two 15½-inch-long pieces and one 7¾-inch-long piece. From the light strip, cut one 15½-inch-long piece and two 7¾-inch-long pieces.

Step 3. To make an A strip set, sew a 15½-inch-long dark strip to each side of a 15½-inch-long light strip, as shown in **Diagram 3.** Press the seams toward the dark strips.

Diagram 3

Step 4. Square up one end of the strip set. Cut 1½-inch-wide segments from the set, as shown in **Diagram 4.** You should be able to cut ten segments.

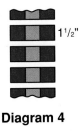

Diagram 4

Step 5. To make a B strip set, sew a 7¾-inch-long light strip to each side of a 7¾-inch-long dark strip, as shown in **Diagram 5** on page 74. Press the seams toward the dark strip. Use your rotary-cutting equipment to square up one end of the set. You should be able to cut five 1½-inch segments from it, as shown.

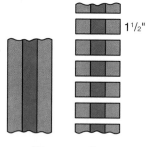

Diagram 5

Step 6. For the corner Nine Patch blocks, sew an A segment to each side of a B segment, as shown in **Diagram 6A**. Press.

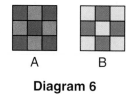

Diagram 6

Step 7. For the center Nine Patch blocks, repeat Steps 2 through 5, reversing the use of light and dark fabrics. Sew a B segment to each side of an A segment, as shown in **6B**.

Step 8. Continue assembling blocks until you have sewn the total number of corner and center Nine Patch blocks required for your quilt size.

ASSEMBLING THE DOUBLE NINE PATCH BLOCKS

Step 1. Lay out five Nine Patch blocks and four gray setting squares into three rows, as shown in **Diagram 7**, placing the light-colored center Nine Patch block in the center. Sew the blocks into rows. Press the seams toward the setting squares.

Step 2. Sew the rows together, matching the seams carefully. Press.

Step 3. Repeat until you have assembled the required number of Double Nine Patch blocks for your quilt.

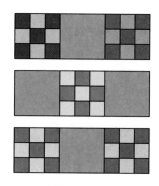

Diagram 7

ASSEMBLING THE QUILT TOP

Step 1. Use a design wall to lay out the blocks, setting squares, side setting triangles, and corner triangles, as shown in the **Quilt Diagram** on page 76.

Step 2. Referring to the **Assembly Diagram**, sew the blocks and triangles together in diagonal rows, pressing the seams toward the setting squares and side setting triangles. Sew the rows together, matching seams carefully. Press.

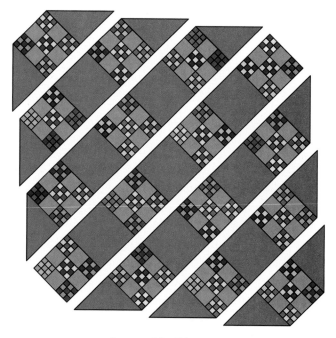

Assembly Diagram

Step 3. Sew a corner triangle to each side of the quilt, matching the mid-point of a triangle's longest side to the midpoint of a block side, as shown by the dashed line in **Diagram 8.** Press seams toward the corner triangles.

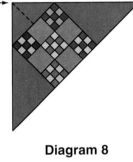

Match centers →

Diagram 8

ASSEMBLING THE INNER BORDERS

Step 1. For each border, assemble diagonal rows by sewing beige side setting triangles to purple squares, as shown in **Diagram 9.** For the bed topper, use 12 dark purple squares along each border; for the king-size quilt, use 18 squares. Press seams toward the purple squares. Sew the rows together, then press all seams in one direction.

Diagram 9

Note: If you are making the bed topper, you may notice that you'll have only 12 triangles along each border instead of the 13 shown in the photograph on page 70. The directions for the border were written to include standard rotary measurements and eliminate the need for odd-size pieces.

Step 2. Sew beige corner triangles to each end of the border strips, as shown in **Diagram 10.** Press.

Diagram 10

Step 3. Fold a border strip in half crosswise and crease. Unfold it and position it right side

down along one side of the quilt, matching the crease to the horizontal midpoint. Pin at the midpoint and ends first, then across the entire width of the quilt. The width of each quilt block should correspond to the width of three purple squares in the border. Sew the border to the quilt, then press the seam toward the quilt. Repeat on the opposite side of the quilt.

Step 4. Sew a 4¾-inch red corner square to each end of the two remaining borders, as shown in **Diagram 11.** Press seams toward the red squares.

Diagram 11

Step 5. Sew the top and bottom borders to the quilt in the same manner as for the side borders.

ADDING THE OUTER BORDER

Step 1. Measure the length of the quilt top, taking the measurement through the vertical center of the quilt rather than along its sides. Cut or piece two borders this exact length from the green border strips.

Step 2. Sew the side borders to the quilt in the same manner as the inner side borders, pinning at the middle and ends first, then along the entire length of the side. Ease in fullness as necessary. Press the seam toward the green border.

Step 3. Measure the width of the quilt top, taking the measurement through the horizontal center of the quilt and stopping at the seam for the outer side borders. Add ½ inch to the measurement, and cut or piece two border strips this exact length from the green border strips.

Step 4. Sew a 12¼-inch red corner square to each end of the top and bottom border strips. Press the seams toward the green border.

Step 5. Sew the top and bottom borders to the quilt in the same manner as the side borders.

QUILTING AND FINISHING

Step 1. Mark the quilt top for quilting. The quilt shown uses cross-hatching in the Double Nine Patch blocks, a feathered circle for the setting squares, a flower in the purple border squares, and a feathered swirl in the outer border.

Step 2. Cut the backing fabric crosswise into three equal pieces, and trim the selvages. For the bed topper, cut 25-inch-wide segments from two of the pieces, and sew one of these narrow segments to each side of the full-width piece, as shown in **Diagram 12.** For the king-size quilt, cut 39-inch-wide segments from two of the pieces, and sew a narrow segment to each side of the full-width piece, as shown. Press seams open.

Step 3. Layer the quilt top, batting, and backing, and baste the layers together. Quilt as desired.

Step 4. Referring to the directions on page 121, make and attach double-fold binding to finish 1 inch wide, cutting the binding strips 4½ inches wide. To calculate the amount of binding needed for the quilt size you are making, add the length of the four sides of the quilt, plus 9 inches.

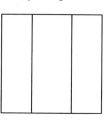

Diagram 12

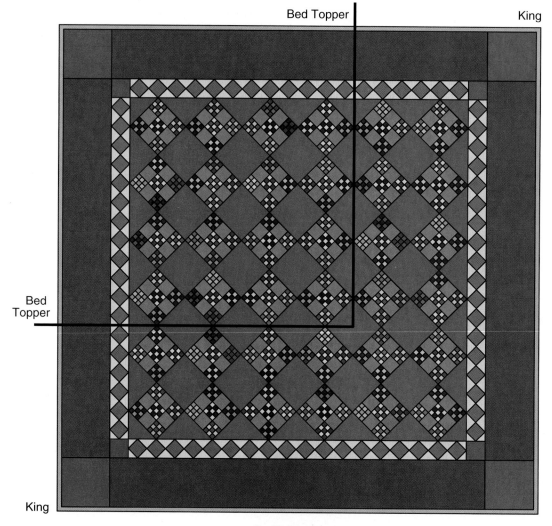

Quilt Diagram

DOUBLE NINE PATCH
Color Plan

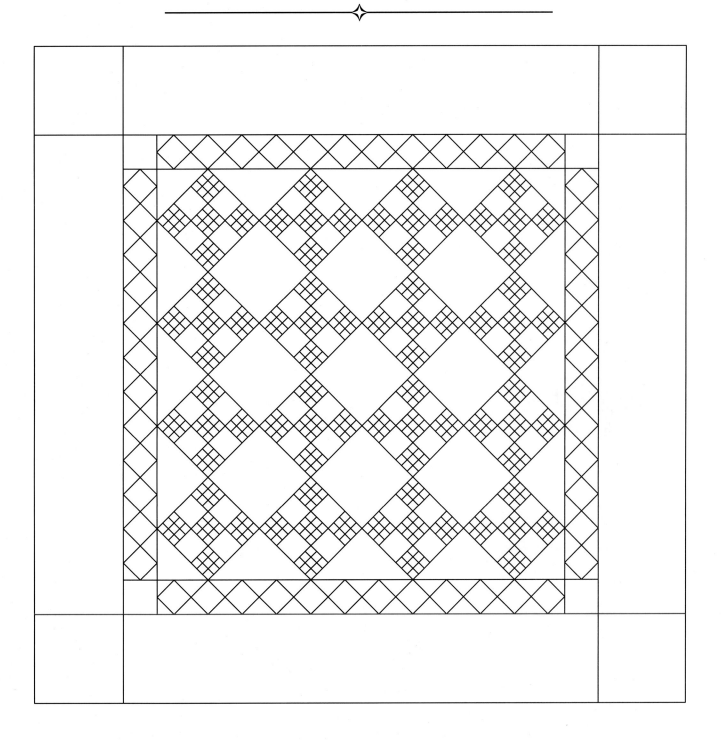

Photocopy this page and use it to experiment with color schemes for your quilt.

SPARKLE PLENTY

Skill Level: *Challenging*

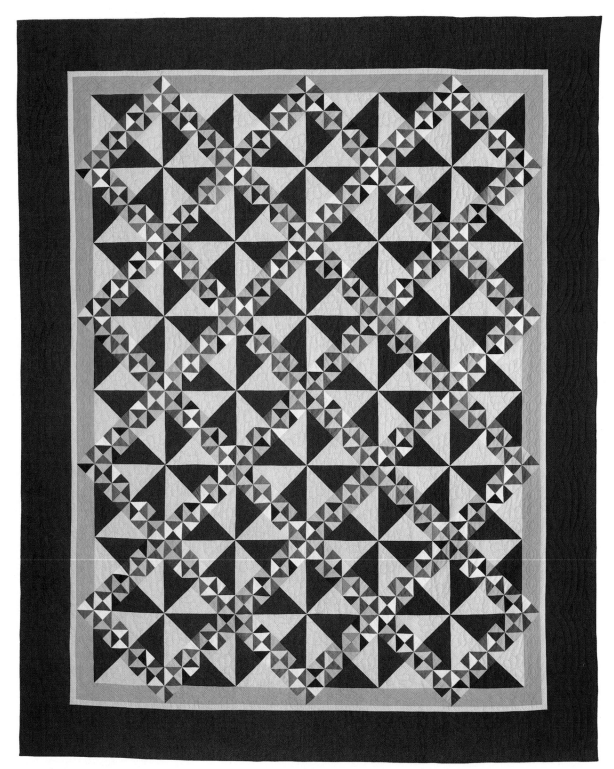

Sparkling Amish solids color this contemporary Amish-look quilt. Quiltmaker Joan Dyer of Redondo Beach, California, was inspired by a 1930s-era pinwheel quilt and chose orchid and navy to flavor her version of large and small pinwheels. Joan made this queen-size quilt as a wedding gift for her eldest daughter, but the directions also include a wallhanging that is equally suitable for gift giving.

BEFORE YOU BEGIN

Triangle squares are used to assemble the large, on-point orchid and navy pinwheel blocks and the multicolored pinwheel block sashing that surrounds them.

Two quick-piecing methods are described on pages 107–109. The large pinwheels are assembled using the single square method. The single square method and the grid method are both suitable for the small pinwheels. **We recommend you read the instructions for both methods before choosing fabrics or starting this project.**

CHOOSING FABRICS

To make a quilt similar to the one shown, choose light orchid and navy fabrics for the large pinwheel blocks. The light orchid fabric is repeated in the middle border, the navy in the wide, outer border. A medium orchid fabric is used in the inner border.

In the quilt shown, the quiltmaker used many subdued Amish colors in the small pinwheels, but added sparkle by scattering an occasional vivid dark or light solid

Quilt Sizes

	Wallhanging	Queen (shown)
Finished Quilt Size	70¼" × 70¼"	93" × 115½"
Finished Block Size		
Large Pinwheel	12"	12"
Small Pinwheel	4"	4"
Number of Blocks		
Large Pinwheel	5	18
Large Half-Pinwheel	4	10
Small Pinwheel	60	175
Number of Triangle Squares		
Large Pinwheel	20	72
Large Half-Pinwheel	4	10
Small Pinwheel	240	700

Materials

	Wallhanging	Queen
Navy	2¾ yards	5¼ yards
Light orchid	1⅛ yards	3 yards
Medium orchid	1⅛ yards	1½ yards
Assorted darks	1⅛ yards	2¼ yards
Assorted lights and medium lights	1⅛ yards	2¼ yards
Backing	4½ yards	8½ yards
Batting	77" × 77"	99" × 122"
Binding	⅝ yard	⅞ yard

NOTE: Yardages are based on 44/45-inch-wide fabrics that are at least 42 inches wide after preshrinking.

Cutting Chart

Fabric	Used For	Strip Width	Number to Cut Wallhanging	Queen
Navy	Large pinwheels	6⅞"	2	6
	Corners and half-pinwheels	9¾"	1	4
	Outer border	9"	7	11
Light orchid	Large pinwheels	6⅞"	2	6
	Corners and half-pinwheels	9¾"	1	4
	Middle border	1½"	6	9
Medium orchid	Inner border corners	3⅜"	4	4
	Inner border half-pinwheels	3⅜"	4	10
Assorted colors	Small pinwheels	See "Making the Small Pinwheels"		

throughout the blocks. For the small pinwheels, select a variety of solids, half of them dark shades, the rest light to medium-light in value.

Collect as many colors as possible to re-create the sparkling effect of the pinwheels. For example, the yardage requirement for the assorted dark solids for the wallhanging is 1⅛ yards. Buy ⅛ yard of nine different dark fabrics to get the most impact for your money. For the queen size, quarter-yard cuts of fabric will be more economical. Buy ¼ yard of nine different dark solids to reach the 2¼ yards needed.

To help you create your own unique color scheme, photocopy the **Color Plan** on page 87, and use crayons or colored pencils to experiment with different color arrangements.

CUTTING

All measurements include ¼-inch seam allowances. Referring to the Cutting Chart, cut the required number of strips in the widths needed. Cut all strips across the fabric width.

The inner border pieces are cut from strips. When you have cut the number of strips listed in the Cutting Chart, refer to the instructions here to cut the individual pieces. Refer to "Making the Small Pinwheels" to cut the small pinwheel blocks.

• Cut the 6⅞-inch navy and light orchid strips into 6⅞-inch squares.

• Cut the 9¾-inch navy and light orchid strips into 9¾-inch squares.

• Cut the 3⅜-inch medium orchid inner border corner strips into 15⅜-inch lengths.

• Cut the 3⅜-inch medium orchid inner border half-pinwheel strips into 23⅞-inch lengths.

Note: Cut and piece one sample pinwheel in each size before cutting all of the fabric for the quilt.

MAKING THE LARGE PINWHEELS

Each large pinwheel block is made up of four triangle squares, as illustrated below.

Large Pinwheel Block Diagram

Step 1. Refer to the Quilt Sizes chart on page 81 to determine the number of large triangle squares and pinwheel blocks you need for your quilt size. Refer to "Method 2: Single Squares" on page 109 to make the triangle squares for your quilt, using the 6⅞-inch navy and light orchid squares. Press the seams and trim the tips as shown in the basic instructions.

Step 2. Position four of the large triangle squares as shown in **Diagram 1A,** then sew pairs together as indicated. Press the center seam in each pair in opposite directions, then match the seams carefully and sew the two units together. Leave the final seam unpressed for now. The finished block should look like **1B.** Repeat to make the number of whole blocks required. (You will have triangle-squares left over; set them aside. They will be used to assemble the half-pinwheel blocks.)

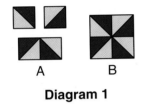

Diagram 1

MAKING THE HALF-PINWHEELS

Step 1. Cut the 9¾-inch light orchid and navy squares in half diagonally twice, as shown in **Diagram 2.**

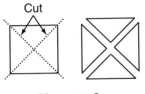

Diagram 2

Step 2. Use one of the leftover orchid/navy triangle squares for each half-pinwheel block. Position the triangle square, an orchid triangle, and a navy triangle, as shown in **Diagram 3.** Be sure to match the edges of the triangles with the triangle squares as shown, then sew them together. Press the seams toward the navy fabric. Set aside the leftover navy and orchid triangles to be used in the quilt's corners.

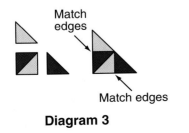

Diagram 3

PREPARING THE INNER BORDERS

Step 1. Fold each 3⅜ × 23⅞-inch medium orchid strip in half crosswise, wrong sides together, matching the edges exactly. Press the strip to mark the center and help the edges adhere to each other. Use your rotary cutter and ruler to make a 45-degree cut across the ends opposite the folds, beginning precisely at the lower corner of the strip, as shown in **Diagram 4.** Open the strip. Repeat for all of the strips.

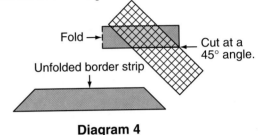

Diagram 4

Step 2. Sew a medium-orchid strip to each large half-pinwheel block, matching the center crease to the center of the pinwheel block (see **Diagram 5**). Press the seam toward the border strip. Repeat for the remaining half-pinwheels.

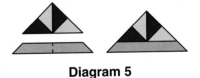

Diagram 5

MAKING THE SMALL PINWHEELS

Each small pinwheel block is made up of four triangle squares, as shown below.

Small Pinwheel Block Diagram

Step 1. Refer to the Quilt Sizes chart on page 81 to determine the number of triangle squares you need to make the small pinwheel blocks. For good contrast, be sure each triangle square pairs a dark fabric with a light or medium-light fabric. To make triangle squares, refer to the assembly methods on pages 107–109. If you are using the grid method, use a 2⅞-inch grid, and cut each piece of yardage in half lengthwise twice so you are working with pieces about 10 inches wide to keep the grid at a manageable size. If using the single square method, cut 2⅞-inch squares.

Step 2. Select four triangle squares and position them with the dark triangles oriented as shown in **Diagram 1** on page 81. Sew the blocks together and press in the same manner as for the large pinwheel blocks, leaving the final seam unpressed.

ASSEMBLING THE CORNER UNITS

Step 1. Fold each 3⅜ × 15⅜-inch medium orchid strip in half and make a 45-degree cut through the ends as described in Step 1 of "Preparing the Inner Borders."

Step 2. Match the centers and sew a trimmed border strip to the longest side of a light orchid triangle to create one-half of a corner unit, as shown in **Diagram 6.** Press the seam toward the border strip. Repeat for the three remaining light orchid triangles. Sew a trimmed border strip to each navy triangle to create the other half of a corner unit, pressing the seam toward the navy triangle.

Step 3. Sew the light orchid and navy units together in pairs, as shown in **Diagram 7.** Make four corner units, matching the seams carefully where border strips meet. Press seams toward the navy unit.

Diagram 6   **Diagram 7**

ASSEMBLING THE QUILT

Step 1. Use a design wall or a flat surface to lay out the quilt in diagonal rows, as shown in the **Wallhanging Assembly Diagram** or the **Queen-**

Size Assembly Diagram. Reposition and rotate the small pinwheels until you're satisfied with the appearance of the quilt; be sure to keep all the dark colors in the same position when rearranging, and avoid positioning light orchid and navy fabrics against their counterpart panels in the large blocks.

Wallhanging Assembly Diagram

Step 2. Assemble the components of the diagonal rows by first sewing together each group of three small pinwheels that separates the large pinwheels. As you align each group for stitching, press the seams that were previously left unpressed so that adjoining blocks have seams facing in opposite directions. Sew the three-pinwheel strips to the sides of the large pinwheels, matching the center and end points carefully, as shown in **Diagram 8.** Press the seams toward the sashing strips.

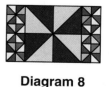

Diagram 8

Step 3. Sew together the long rows of small pinwheels to create sashing strips that separate the diagonal rows of blocks. For the wallhanging, you'll have two rows of five small pinwheels, and two rows of 13 small pinwheels. For the queen size, you will have two rows of five small pinwheels, two rows of 13 small pinwheels, two rows of 21 small pinwheels, and one row of 25 small pinwheels.

Step 4. For the wallhanging, work from the upper left corner and sew the first sashing strip, made of five small pinwheels, to the pinwheel block with sashing. Sew the half-pinwheels to the ends of the pinwheel block row. Sew the corner pinwheel on last. Press. Repeat for the lower right corner. For the center row, sew the long sashing strip to the sides of the pinwheel block row. Sew the upper left and lower right units to the center row, then sew on the corner setting triangles. Press.

Step 5. For the queen size, work from the upper left corner and sew the first sashing strip to the pinwheel block with sashing. Sew the half-pinwheels to the ends of the pinwheel block row. Sew on the corner pinwheel, matching the center point to the center of the adjoining sashing strip.

Queen-Size Assembly Diagram

Press. Sew the next two rows of sashing strips and pinwheel blocks together, matching the seams carefully and pressing them toward the sashing strips. Sew the half-pinwheels to the ends of each row to create the upper left unit. Repeat to assemble the lower right unit of the quilt.

Sew the largest sashing row to the bottom of the upper left corner. Sew the two assembled units together. Sew on the remaining corner pinwheels, matching the center points to the centers of the adjoining sashing strip. Press.

ATTACHING THE BORDERS

Step 1. Measure the quilt top vertically through the center. To this measurement add two times the finished width of the middle border, plus 5 inches (add a total of 7 inches), to allow for the miter. Use the 1½-inch-wide light orchid strips to assemble two side borders this length. Then measure the quilt top horizontally through the center and use the remaining 1½-inch-wide light orchid strips to assemble top and bottom borders this exact length.

Step 2. Pin and sew the four border strips to the quilt top, beginning and ending the seams ¼ inch from the edge of the quilt. Press the seams toward the border. For instructions on mitering, refer to page 119.

Step 3. Add the side outer borders first (see the **Queen-Size Quilt Diagram**). Measure the quilt top vertically through the center. Use the 9-inch-wide navy strips to make two border strips this length.

Step 4. Fold a strip in half crosswise and crease. Unfold it and position it right side down along one side of the quilt, with the crease at the vertical midpoint. Pin at the midpoint and ends first, then along the length of the entire side, easing in fullness. Sew the border to the quilt top. Repeat on the opposite side of the quilt.

Step 5. Measure the width of the quilt top through the horizontal center of the quilt, including side borders. Use the remaining 9-inch navy strips to assemble two strips this exact length. Sew to the top and bottom of the quilt as described in Step 4.

Queen-Size Quilt Diagram

QUILTING AND FINISHING

Step 1. Mark the quilt top for quilting. The quilt shown features a feather wreath in each large pinwheel block, a cable design in the inner borders, and a floral design in the outer borders. Individual patches were quilted in the ditch.

Step 2. To make the backing for the wallhanging, cut the fabric crosswise into two equal pieces, and trim the selvages. Cut one of the pieces in half lengthwise and sew one half to each side of the full-width piece, as shown in **Diagram 9**. Press the seams open. For the queen-size quilt, cut the backing fabric crosswise into three equal pieces, and trim the selvages. Sew the pieces together lengthwise. Press the seams open.

Step 3. Layer the quilt top, batting, and backing. Baste the layers together and quilt as desired.

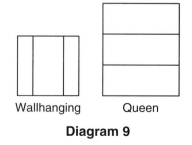

Wallhanging   Queen

Diagram 9

Step 4. Referring to the directions on page 121, make and attach double-fold binding. To calculate the amount of binding needed for the quilt size you are making, add the length of the four sides of the quilt, plus 9 inches.

SPARKLE PLENTY
Color Plan

Photocopy this page and use it to experiment with color schemes for your quilt.

Sunshine and Shadow

Skill Level: *Easy*

*T*he Sunshine and Shadow quilts made by the Amish epitomize their view that nothing should go to waste. Many quilt patterns were adopted or developed by Amish quiltmakers to use up tiny bits of fabric left over from dressmaking. This 1940s-era Lancaster County, Pennsylvania, example juxtaposes lights and darks to create the shadows that give the pattern its name. The quilt is part of a collection owned by Douglas Tompkins of Puerto Montt, Chile.

BEFORE YOU BEGIN

The diagonal setting of colors makes this quilt look intricate, but actually it is very easy to piece. Quick-piecing methods are used to construct six different strip sets. Segments are cut from the sets, then arranged into vertical rows to create the design. Individual squares are used to fill in the outer edges of the quilt.

Both quilt sizes are assembled using the same layout and instructions. The strip sizes are the only things that differ.

CHOOSING FABRICS

This quilt contains cool and warm colors in many values. Many colors appear in more than one shade, and, in some cases, gradations of the same color are sewn side by side to form subtly changing diagonal rows. The very dark rows that surround the quilt's center set off the central motif.

To help create your own unique color scheme, photocopy the **Color Plan** on page 93, and use crayons or colored pencils to ex-

Quilt Sizes

	Wallhanging	Queen (shown)
Finished Quilt Size	48½" × 48½"	86¾" × 86¾"
Size of Squares	1"	1¾"
Number of Squares	841	841

Materials

	Wallhanging	Queen
Bubblegum pink	1¼ yards	2¼ yards
Cranberry	1⅛ yards	2¾ yards
Red	⅜ yard	⅝ yard
Black	⅜ yard	¾ yard
Grape	⅜ yard	½ yard
Purple	¼ yard	½ yard
Yellow, wine, tan, denim blue, and dark red	¼ yard *each*	⅜ yard *each*
Light blue and royal	⅛ yard *each*	¼ yard *each*
Copper and lilac	⅛ yard *each*	⅜ yard *each*
Dark teal, teal, and turquoise	⅛ yard *each*	¼ yard *each*
Deep purple	⅛ yard	⅛ yard
Backing	3¼ yards	8 yards
Batting	54" × 54"	93" × 93"
Binding	½ yard	¾ yard

NOTE: Yardages are based on 44/45-inch-wide fabrics that are at least 42 inches wide after preshrinking.

Cutting Chart					
		Wallhanging		Queen	
Fabric	Used For	Strip Width	Number to Cut	Strip Width	Number to Cut
Bubblegum pink	Inner border	3"	4	4¾"	6
	Border corner squares	7¼"	1	13¼	2
	Strip sets	1½"	8	2¼"	8
Cranberry	Squares and strip sets	1½"	3	2¼"	3
	Outer border	7¼"	4	13¼"	6
Red	Squares and strip sets	1½"	5	2¼"	7
Black	Squares and strip sets	1½"	7	2¼"	9
Grape	Squares and strip sets	1½"	5	2¼"	6
Purple	Strip sets	1½"	5	2¼"	5
Yellow	Squares and strip sets	1½"	3	2¼"	4
Wine	Strip sets	1½"	3	2¼"	4
Tan	Strip sets	1½"	3	2¼"	4
Denim blue	Squares and strip sets	1½"	4	2¼"	4
Dark red	Strip sets	1½"	3	2¼"	3
Light blue	Strip sets	1½"	2	2¼"	2
Royal	Strip sets	1½"	2	2¼"	2
Copper	Strip sets	1½"	2	2¼"	3
Lilac	Strip sets	1½"	2	2¼"	3
Dark teal	Strip sets	1½"	1	2¼"	2
Teal	Strip sets	1½"	1	2¼"	2
Turquoise	Strip sets	1½"	1	2¼"	2
Deep purple	Strip sets	1½"	1	2¼"	1

periment with different color arrangements. For a glowing effect, try coloring squares diagonally, but creating rows that are three squares across. Move from dark to light in the first three blocks and from light to dark in the next three, as shown in the **Light and Dark Color Plan** on page 92.

CUTTING

All measurements include ¼-inch seam allowances. Refer to the Cutting Chart for the number, color, and dimensions of strips required for your quilt size.

Make the border corner squares for the wallhanging by cutting the 7¼-inch bubblegum pink strip into four 7¼-inch squares, and for the queen-size quilt by cutting the 13¼-inch bubblegum pink strips into four 13¼-inch squares.

To make the individual squares for the wallhanging, cut only one of the 1½-inch strips of each of the following colors into 1½-inch squares: cranberry, red, black, yellow, grape, and denim blue. Do not cut the remaining strips in those colors into squares. To make the individual squares for the queen-size quilt, cut only one of the 2¼-inch strips into 2¼-inch squares in the same colors. Do not cut the remaining strips in those colors into squares.

Note: Piece and cut one sample strip set before cutting all the fabric for the quilt. After

you have assembled your strip set, check it for accuracy before cutting it into segments.

MAKING THE STRIP SETS

You may find it helpful to refer to the **Fabric Key** as you make your strip sets to be sure you are selecting the correct color fabrics.

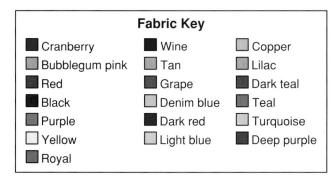

Fabric Key

- Cranberry
- Bubblegum pink
- Red
- Black
- Purple
- Yellow
- Royal
- Wine
- Tan
- Grape
- Denim blue
- Dark red
- Light blue
- Copper
- Lilac
- Dark teal
- Teal
- Turquoise
- Deep purple

Step 1. Make strip set 1 by sewing strips together lengthwise in the color order shown in **Diagram 1**. Press all seams in one direction.

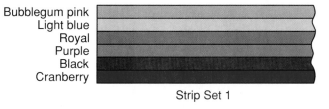

Bubblegum pink
Light blue
Royal
Purple
Black
Cranberry

Strip Set 1

Diagram 1

Step 2. Use your rotary equipment to square up one end of the strip set. Cut as many segments from the strip set as possible, as shown in **Diagram 2**. For the wallhanging, cut 1½-inch segments; for the queen-size quilt, cut 2¼-inch segments. Repeat until you have 28 segments. Label and set them aside.

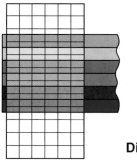

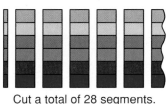

Cut a total of 28 segments.

Diagram 2

Step 3. Referring to **Diagram 3** for color order and segment quantities, assemble strip sets 2 through 6. Sew the strips in each set together in the same manner as for strip set 1, and press all of the seams in one direction. Follow the directions in Step 2 to square up and cut the segments.

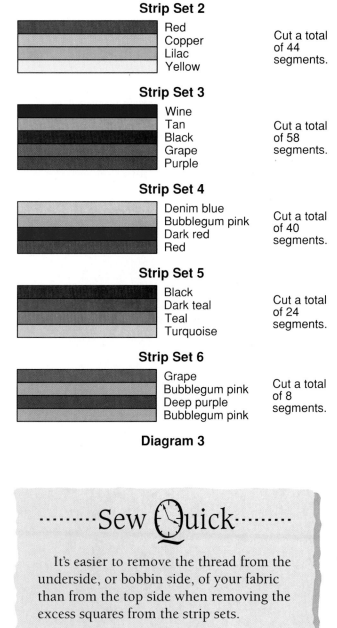

Strip Set 2

Red
Copper
Lilac
Yellow

Cut a total of 44 segments.

Strip Set 3

Wine
Tan
Black
Grape
Purple

Cut a total of 58 segments.

Strip Set 4

Denim blue
Bubblegum pink
Dark red
Red

Cut a total of 40 segments.

Strip Set 5

Black
Dark teal
Teal
Turquoise

Cut a total of 24 segments.

Strip Set 6

Grape
Bubblegum pink
Deep purple
Bubblegum pink

Cut a total of 8 segments.

Diagram 3

········ Sew Quick ········

It's easier to remove the thread from the underside, or bobbin side, of your fabric than from the top side when removing the excess squares from the strip sets.

LAYING OUT THE QUILT TOP

Step 1. Use a design wall or other flat surface to lay out the quilt. The quilt is divided into four quadrants, as shown in the **Layout Diagram.** Begin with any quadrant and align segments vertically, offsetting the squares in adjoining columns to create diagonal bands of color. In some cases, near the top and bottom of a quadrant, you will not need entire segments. When this happens, use a seam ripper to remove the unneeded squares from the end of a segment. Fill in around the edges of the quilt with individual squares, as shown by the circles in the diagram.

Step 2. Referring to the **Piecing Diagram** and working in one quadrant at a time, sew segments and individual squares together in each vertical column. Press seams in adjoining columns in opposite directions before sewing; handle columns carefully to avoid stretching them out of shape.

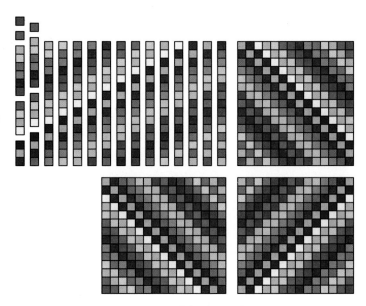

Piecing Diagram

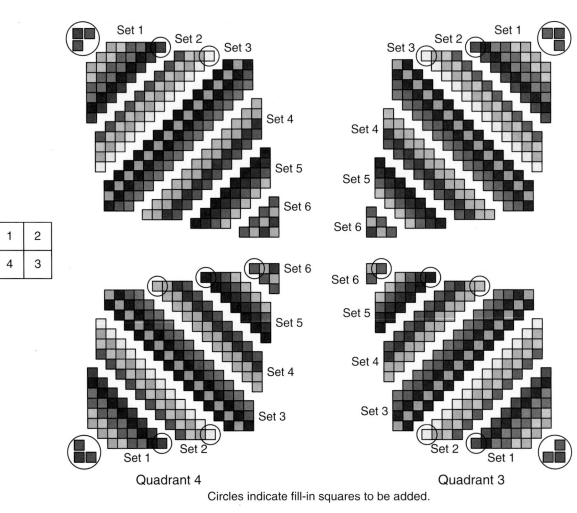

Circles indicate fill-in squares to be added.

Layout Diagram

Step 3. Sew all of the columns of one quadrant together, matching seams carefully. Press the completed quadrant and measure its sides to make sure the unit is square. If it is off slightly, press carefully to square it up. Assemble the remaining three quadrants in the same manner, using the **Layout Diagram** as a guide to segment placement.

Step 4. Sew the two top quadrants together along their inside edges, then do the same for the two bottom quadrants. Sew the two quilt halves together. Press the quilt top and measure its sides to be sure the unit is square. Press again.

ADDING THE INNER BORDER

Step 1. Measure the length of the quilt through the vertical center of the quilt rather than along the edge. Using the inner border strips, cut two borders this exact length, or piece strips together end to end to achieve the required length.

Step 2. Fold one strip in half crosswise and crease. Unfold it and position it right side down along one side of the quilt, with the crease at the horizontal midpoint. Pin at the midpoint and ends first, then along the length of the entire side, easing in fullness as necessary. Sew the border to the quilt. Repeat on the opposite side of the quilt.

Step 3. Measure the width of the quilt through the horizontal center, including the side borders. Cut or piece together inner border strips to make two borders this exact length.

Step 4. In the same manner as for the side borders, pin and sew the top and bottom border strips to the quilt top.

ADDING THE OUTER BORDER

Step 1. Measure the length of the quilt top, including inner borders, through the vertical center of the quilt. Cut or piece together outer border strips to make two side borders this exact length.

Step 2. Sew the outer side borders to the quilt in the same manner as for the inner side borders.

Step 3. Measure the width of the quilt top through the horizontal center of the quilt, stopping at the seams for the outer side borders. Add ½ inch to this measurement, and cut or piece together two outer border strips this exact length for the top and bottom borders.

Step 4. Sew a border corner square to each end of the two border strips, as shown in **Diagram 4**. Press the seams toward the borders.

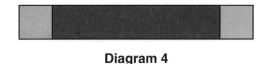

Diagram 4

Step 5. Sew the top and bottom borders to the quilt in the same manner as for the side borders, matching the side border and corner square seams.

QUILTING AND FINISHING

Step 1. Mark the quilt top for quilting. The quilt shown has a diagonal grid through the center, a flowering vine in the inner border, and basket motifs in the outer border and corner squares.

Step 2. To make the backing for the wall-hanging, cut the backing fabric in half crosswise and trim the selvages. Cut a 15-inch-wide panel from one piece, and sew it to the full-width piece, as shown in **Diagram 5**. Press the seam open.

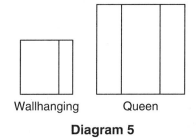

Wallhanging　　Queen

Diagram 5

Step 3. To make the backing for the queen-size quilt, cut the backing fabric crosswise into three equal pieces. Cut 27-inch-wide panels from two of

Quilt Diagram

the pieces, and sew a narrow panel to each side of the full-width piece, as shown in the diagram. Press the seams open.

Step 4. Layer the quilt top, batting, and backing. Baste the layers together and quilt as desired.

Step 5. Referring to the directions on page 121, make and attach double-fold binding. For the wallhanging, make binding to finish at a width of ½ inch. For the queen-size quilt, make binding to finish at a width of 1 inch. To calculate the amount of binding needed for the quilt size you are making, add the length of the four sides of the quilt, plus 9 inches.

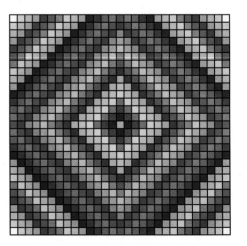

Light and Dark Color Plan

SUNSHINE AND SHADOW
Color Plan

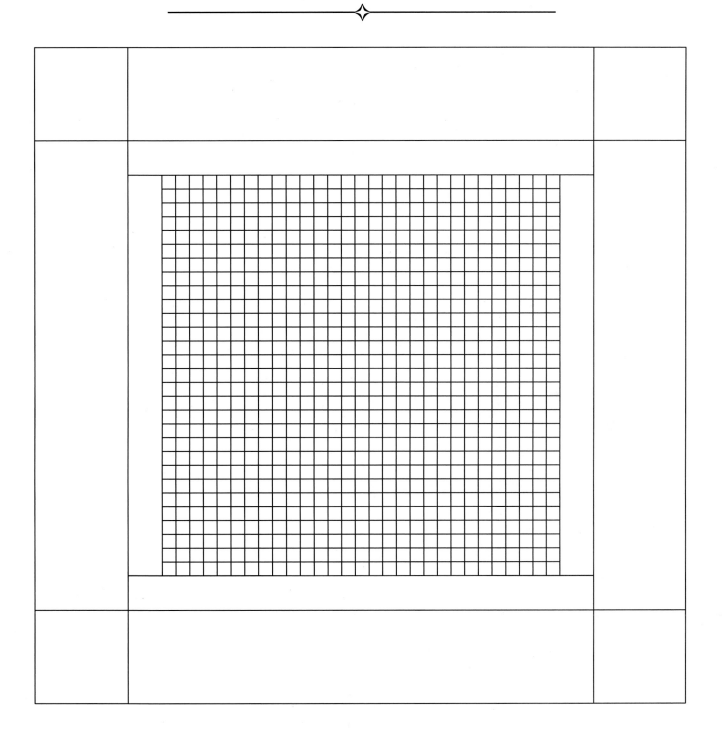

Photocopy this page and use it to experiment with color schemes for your quilt.

ROMAN STRIPE

Skill Level: *Easy*

Typically associated with the midwestern Amish, this Roman Stripe pattern was pieced with darker colors set against black. The popularity of strip-pieced patchwork, like the Roman Stripe or Log Cabin, hit its peak in the first 20 years of this century. Part of the Esprit Collection owned by Susie Tompkins, the quilt has been traced back to 1925 and Holmes County, Ohio.

BEFORE YOU BEGIN

The striped portions of the blocks in this quilt are assembled using a quick-piecing technique. Long strips of fabric are sewn together lengthwise to make strip sets, then a cutting guide is used to cut five triangles from each set. To complete a block, a striped triangle is sewn to a solid black triangle.

The inner, pieced border is assembled from small triangle squares cut from templates A and B. To avoid odd-size rotary-cutting dimensions, the zigzag border given is a slight deviation from the one used in the quilt shown and can be most accurately cut using templates.

CHOOSING FABRICS

Seven strip sets are used to assemble the blocks for this quilt, and each set contains five different fabrics. Each strip set will produce triangles with two color placement variations. Choose at least five different fabric colors to make the striped units. If purchasing more than five colors, buy fabric in ⅛-yard cuts for the greatest variety. The quilt shown contains fabrics varying from light to dark in value.

CUTTING

All measurements include ¼-inch seam allowances unless otherwise noted. The pieces are cut using a combination of rotary-cutting techniques and templates. Using the rotary cutter, cut an 80-inch-long black piece for the outer borders first, cutting on the lengthwise grain to minimize seams. Then cut the required number of lengthwise strips in the width needed from the 80-inch-long black piece. You'll cut these border strips to the exact length needed once the quilt top is assembled.

After you have finished the lengthwise cutting, refer to the Cutting Chart and cut the required number of crosswise strips needed for each color. From the 9⅝-inch black strips, cut 9⅝-inch squares. Cut each square in half once diagonally, as shown in **Diagram 1**.

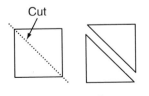

Cut

Diagram 1

Make templates for pieces A and B using the full-size patterns

on page 100, and cut the number of pieces listed in the Cutting Chart. Be sure to position the templates along the fabric's straight of grain as indicated by the arrow on each template. For details on making and using templates, see page 116.

Note: Cut and piece one sample block before cutting all of the fabric for the quilt.

Quilt Size

Finished Quilt Size	68½" × 86"
Finished Block Size	8¾"
Number of Blocks	35

NOTE: Due to the nature of the pieced border, no size variations are provided.

Materials

Black	5¼ yards
Assorted lights to medium darks	1⅞ yards
Rust	1⅛ yards
Backing	5⅝ yards
Batting	75" × 91"
Binding	⅝ yard

NOTE: Yardages are based on 44/45-inch-wide fabrics that are at least 42 inches wide after preshrinking.

Cutting Chart

Fabric	Used For	Lengthwise Strip Width	Number to Cut
Black	Outer borders	10½"	4*

Fabric	Used For	Crosswise Strip Width	Number to Cut
Black	Blocks	9⅝"	5
	A		108
	B		4
Rust	A		96
	B		4
Assorted lights to medium darks	Stripes	1¾"	35

Refer to "Cutting" on page 95 before cutting these strips.

PIECING THE ROMAN STRIPE BLOCKS

Step 1. Select five different color 1¾ × 42-inch strips. Use a scant ¼-inch seam allowance to sew the strips together lengthwise, as shown in **Diagram 2.** Sewing strips together with just slightly less than a ¼-inch seam ensures that the completed strip set will be wide enough to mark and cut triangles on. For best contrast, avoid using very dark fabrics on either outside edge of the strip set, where they would eventually be positioned against the black half of the Roman Stripe block. Press all of the seams in one direction.

Diagram 2

Step 2. To make a cutting guide, draw a 9⅝-inch square on a large piece of paper and cut it in half once diagonally, as shown in **Diagram 3A.** Tape the triangle to the wrong side of a large, square rotary ruler, as shown in **3B,** or make a guide the same size as the paper from any template material.

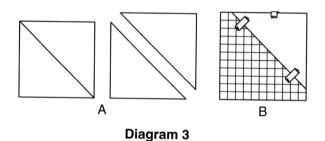

Diagram 3

Step 3. If you're using a ruler and paper as your guide, align the guide with the strip set, placing the long edge of the guide against the bottom of the strip set and the left tip at the left corner of the strip set, as shown in **Diagram 4A.** Use your rotary-cutting equipment to make a 45-degree cut along the right edge of the ruler. To avoid unsafe backward or left-hand cuts, rotate your rotary cutting mat 180 degrees, realign the guide, and make the second cut to complete the triangle, as shown in **4B.** Continue cutting across the width of the strip set, cutting a total of five triangles from the set, as shown in **4C.** This will yield two triangle variations, with stripes in opposite positions. If using a template as a guide, mark both sides of the first triangle, and cut out on the lines. Continue marking and cutting in the same manner to yield five triangles from each strip set.

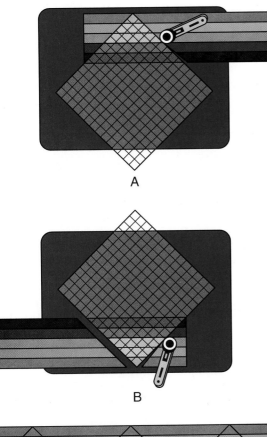

A

B

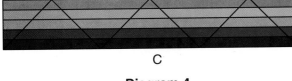

C

Diagram 4

── **Sew Easy** ──

Handle the striped triangles carefully, since their short edges are cut on the fabric's bias. To avoid stretching these edges, sew a stabilizing seam ⅛ inch from each short edge of the triangle before sewing it to the black portion of the block.

ASSEMBLING THE QUILT TOP

Step 1. Use a flat surface to arrange the blocks into seven rows, each containing five blocks, as shown in the **Assembly Diagram.**

Step 4. Make six more strip sets, then cut triangles from the sets in the same manner. Add variety to your blocks by changing the fabric in each set. Cut a total of 35 striped triangles.

Step 5. Align the longest side of a large black triangle with the longest side of a striped triangle and sew the two together, as shown in **Diagram 5.** Press the seam toward the dark triangle. Repeat to assemble all blocks.

Diagram 5

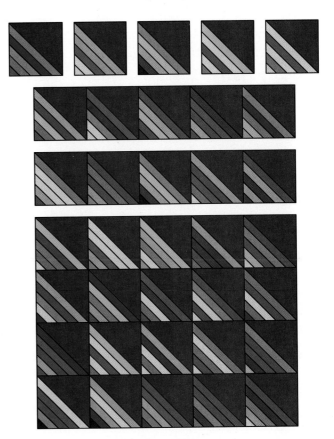

Assembly Diagram

Step 2. Sew the five blocks in each row together. Press seams in adjoining rows in opposite directions, then sew the rows together, matching seam intersections carefully. Press.

For speedy accuracy checks when assembling blocks, place a ruler with a self-stick backing on the table in front of your sewing machine. If you have difficulty finding a self-stick model, make your own with double-sided tape. As you sew, check your block or row size against the ruler to be sure the size is accurate.

ADDING THE PIECED BORDER

The pieced inner border is assembled by sewing two narrow border strips from the black and rust patches cut from templates A and B. The strips are sewn together lengthwise to create the zigzag design.

Step 1. For the inner portion of the top and bottom borders, sew ten black A triangles to nine rust A triangles, as shown in **Diagram 6,** beginning and ending with a black triangle. Press. Make a second, identical strip and set both strips aside.

Diagram 6

Step 2. For the side borders, sew 14 black A triangles to 13 rust A triangles, as shown in **Diagram 7,** beginning and ending the strip with a black triangle. Press. Make a second, identical strip and set both strips aside.

Diagram 7

Step 3. Align the black edge of one of the shorter pieced strips, right side down, along the

top edge of the quilt. Pin and match the middles and ends of the two pieces. Pin along the width of the quilt, matching intersecting seams. Sew the border to the quilt, as shown in **Diagram 8.** Press. Repeat with the second shorter pieced strip on the bottom of the quilt.

Diagram 8

Step 4. Sew the side borders to the quilt in the same manner as the top and bottom borders.

Step 5. To make a border corner unit, sew two black A triangles together along their short sides, as shown in **Diagram 9.** Press. Repeat to make a total of four corner units.

Diagram 9

Step 6. Sew a corner unit to each corner of the quilt, matching the midpoints, as shown in **Diagram 10.** Press.

Diagram 10

Step 7. For the outer portion of the top and bottom borders, sew 11 black A triangles to 10 rust A triangles, as shown in **Diagram 11A,** beginning and ending with a black A triangle. Sew a rust B triangle to each end of the strip, as shown in **11B.** Press. Repeat, making a second identical strip.

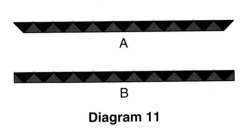

Diagram 11

Step 8. Align the rust edge of one of the strips, right side down, along the top edge of the quilt. Pin and match the middles and ends of the two border pieces. Pin along the entire width of the quilt, easing in any fullness. Be sure the points of the black triangles are aligned with the points of the rust triangles in the first pieced border to form a zigzag pattern. Sew the border to the quilt, as shown in **Diagram 12**. Press. Repeat on the bottom of the quilt.

Diagram 12

Step 9. For the side borders, sew 16 rust A triangles to 15 black A triangles, as shown in **Diagram 13A**, beginning and ending with a rust A triangle. Sew a black B triangle to each end of the strip, as shown in **13B**. Press. Repeat, making a second identical strip.

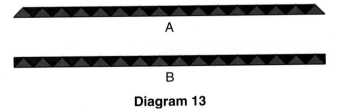

Diagram 13

Step 10. Sew the side borders to the quilt in the same manner as the top and bottom borders, as shown in **Diagram 14**. Be sure the points of the black triangles are aligned with the points of the rust triangles in the first pieced border to form a zigzag pattern. Press.

Diagram 14

ADDING THE OUTER BORDERS

Step 1. Refer to the **Quilt Diagram** to add the outer borders. Measure the length of the quilt, taking the measurement through the vertical center of the quilt rather than along the sides. Cut two black 10½-inch-wide strips this exact length.

Step 2. Fold one strip in half crosswise and crease. Unfold it and position it right side down along one side of the quilt, with the crease at the horizontal midpoint. Pin at the midpoint and ends first, then along the length of the entire side, easing in fullness as necessary. Sew the border to the quilt. Repeat on the opposite side of the quilt. Press the seams toward the borders.

Step 3. Measure the width of the quilt, taking the measurement through the horizontal center of the quilt and including the side borders. Cut two strips this exact length. Sew the top and bottom borders to the quilt in the same manner as the side borders, following the directions in Step 2.

QUILTING AND FINISHING

Step 1. Mark the quilt top for quilting. In the quilt shown, the striped portions of the blocks were quilted in the ditch, and the black portions were quilted in a double crosshatch pattern.

Step 2. Cut the backing fabric into two equal pieces, and trim the selvages. Sew the two pieces together lengthwise, as shown in **Diagram 15** on page 100. Press the seam open.

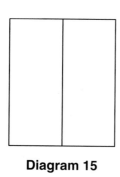

Diagram 15

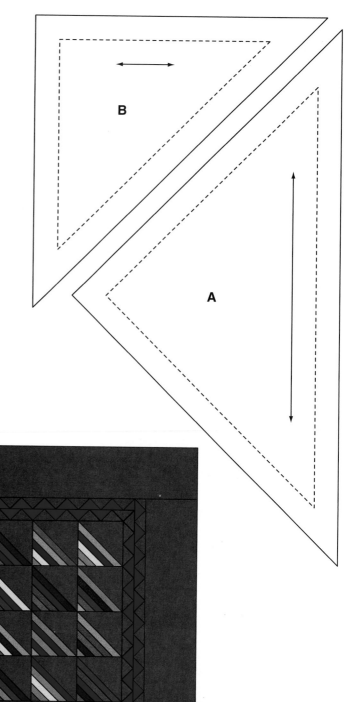

Step 3. Layer the quilt top, batting, and backing, and baste the layers together. Quilt as desired.

Step 4. Referring to the directions on page 121, make and attach double-fold binding. To calculate the amount of binding needed for the quilt, add the length of the four sides, plus 9 inches.

Quilt Diagram

ROMAN STRIPE
Color Plan

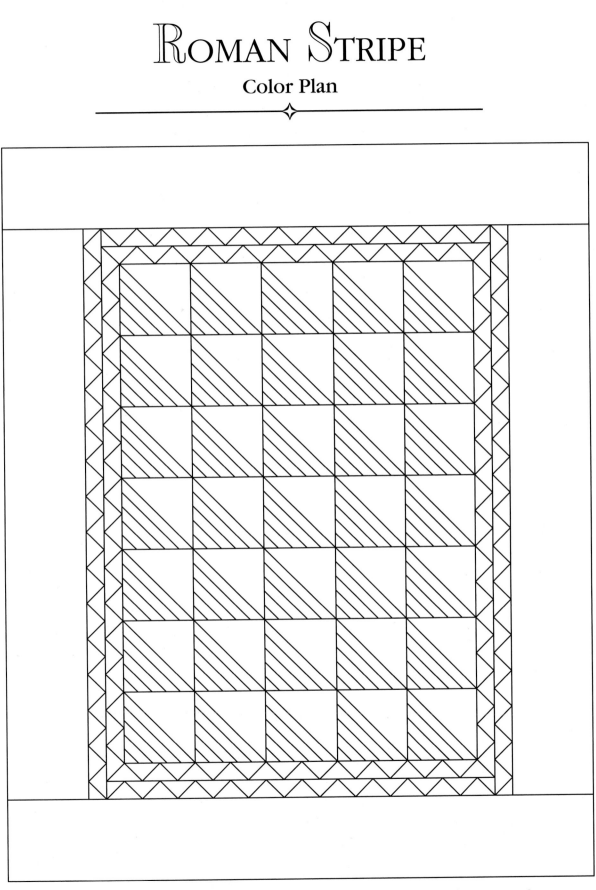

Photocopy this page and use it to experiment with color schemes for your quilt.

AMISH
◇
BASICS

Who Are the Amish?

Although not officially called the Amish until almost 1700, the beliefs and way of life of this religious group began as a result of the Anabaptist movement in sixteenth century Europe. The members of the movement desired a more intense and structured spiritual life than was offered to them by other Protestant religions of the time. They believed that only adults were capable of choosing baptism, or membership, into a specific religion—a drastic departure from a culture that automatically baptized members at birth.

The Anabaptists were persecuted for their beliefs. Although they found relative peace from persecution when they moved into the Rhine Valley, there wasn't any stability in their lives. The state religion of the area changed constantly, depending on who controlled the territory. Their religious freedoms fluctuated, too, and depended upon the tolerance of the current ruler. In a search for freedom, the Amish and members of the closely related Mennonite and Hutterite faiths began to emigrate to America.

Amish Life

The first Amish who arrived in this country were scattered about, and many were eventually absorbed into different faiths. As the number of Amish immigrants grew, however, communities were established and tightly knit groups emerged. Members pooled their resources and worked together to improve the community as a whole. Decisions about every aspect of daily life were made as a group, and that practice continues today. Each Amish community is considered an extended family, and the support the members give each other helps to hold the group together spiritually and eliminate influences from the outside world. Self-sufficiency is important to the Amish, and most modern conveniences are shunned.

Individual communities, or districts, are normally composed of no more than 30 to 40 families. Each district follows the written laws of the Amish faith but leaves many details open to interpretation, including the use of color in clothing,

quilts, and other everyday items. However, life among members of a specific district is standardized. Men wear the same types of pants and shirts, women wear the same dresses and bonnets, members drive the same color and type of buggies, and homes are furnished in very similar manners. Each district has its own identity, and those who wish to stay within that community must abide by the decisions of the group. When a family moves into a new district, they stop using all items that do not conform with the customs of the new group. This may mean that clothing styles or colors are changed, or that an unsuitable quilt must be put or given away.

Quiltmaking among the Amish

In the past, many Amish districts had no rules regarding the use of color in quilts, while in other districts certain colors, such as pink or white, were not accepted. In some districts, colors considered improper for wearing apparel were not banned from quilts. Some groups felt that too much patchwork was improper, since it wasn't really required to make a functional quilt or bed covering. In general, the types of quilts that were considered acceptable were a reflection of the conservative or liberal beliefs of each district. Today, a great number of Amish quilts are made for resale outside the Amish community, so the use of color and pattern is not as limited as it was in the past.

After studying records of household inventories from the nineteenth century, historians generally agree that quilting probably did not become an important skill in the Amish household until the late 1880s. The few remaining examples of early Amish quilts from the period prior to the 1870s are closely quilted whole-cloth works. Simple patchwork patterns, such as Nine Patch and Center Diamond, began to emerge after this time.

Although homespun fabric was occasionally used, most early Amish quilts were sewn from mass-produced cottons and wools colored with natural dyes in shades of indigo, green, tan, brown, rust, red, and yellow. Later, as synthetic dyes became widely used, Amish women introduced brighter colors into their quilts.

REGIONAL DIFFERENCES

Amish quilt styles varied across the United States just as they did from district to district. One of the oldest and most prosperous Amish communities is in Lancaster County, Pennsylvania. In the past, quilts made in this area had several distinctive characteristics. They were usually square and had very wide borders, often with corner blocks. Wide bindings were also common. Diamond in a Square, Bars and Split Bars, Sunshine and Shadow, Nine Patch variations, and Baskets were all popular patterns, and most were heavily quilted. Prior to World War II, most Lancaster quilts were sewn with lightweight woolens. After that time, woolens were more expensive and harder to obtain, so a variety of natural and synthetic fabrics were used. Printed fabric is rarely seen in Amish quilts, but in Lancaster County it was often used for the backing. Lancaster quiltmakers worked with an extensive color palette, generally shying away from white and yellow as "unsuitable" colors. The variety of colors used grew as new colors became more available in the marketplace. Black did not appear as often in Lancaster County quilts as it did in other Amish areas.

Quilts made by the Ohio Amish were usually more intricately pieced than those made in Lancaster. Geometric blocks were popular, and different patterns were often combined, allowing the quiltmaker more originality in her design. Pieced borders and bindings were common, and some quilts were reversible. In Ohio, cotton sateens and fine cottons (when sateens were no longer available) were the preferred fabrics. Backings were usually solid and were made in any color, including white. Intricate quilting motifs were generally reserved for open border areas. All colors were used and, as in other areas, the use of colors became more diverse as the marketplace grew. Black became a popular choice for backgrounds and borders during the 1920s. Although the patchwork is not as intricate, quilts made by Amish women in Indiana and Illinois are similar to those made in Ohio.

In Iowa, it was not unusual to find a small amount of print fabric in the quilt top. White, pink, and other pastels were also used. As the Amish moved westward, they took many of the quilting traditions from their eastern districts to their new homes.

In some areas, purchasing fabric specifically for patchwork was either not allowed or was frowned upon. In those areas, patchwork was generally a reflection of the colors and fabrics used for clothing and other necessary items, since a woman's scrap bag was her primary source of quilting supplies. Backings were often purchased for a specific quilt, so in many cases a quilt's age can be determined in part by attempting to date that fabric.

SELECTING COLORS

Historical Perspective

When creating an Amish-style quilt, choose only solid colors. If you would like to make a quilt that is historically accurate for a specific community and era, visit a library to research the patterns, colors, fabrics, and other key elements commonly used in the area and time period you have chosen. Look for books that focus on Amish quilting and others, such as state quilting project books, that might include helpful photos and quilt descriptions. Annual calendars are another source of excellent photographs, and most list the origins of each quilt. You'll find quilt-related calendars in quilt and fabric shops, bookstores, and card and gift shops.

Updating Tradition

To duplicate one of the Amish or Amish-style quilts from this book, take the book with you when purchasing fabric and refer to the color photographs as you make selections. Do not underbuy yardage when selecting solid fabrics, because dye lots vary greatly. It will be practically impossible to match a solid color if you run out while making your quilt.

To make a quilt in the Amish tradition but in keeping with your own needs, choose colors that appeal to you without worrying about whether they are historically correct. Most quilters think of Amish quilts as dark and somber, but a great number of them are very bright and colorful. If you aren't sure where to start when selecting a color scheme, visit your local quilt shop and ask for advice or browse through quilting magazines for inspiration. Many mail-order sources offer assortments of Amish solids in several yardage cuts. These groupings are a good way to familiarize yourself with the variety of solid fabrics that can be included in an Amish quilt.

The Importance of Value

For many designs, such as Sunshine and Shadow and Broken Dishes, color value, or the lightness or darkness of fabrics, is an important consideration. There may be times you choose to ignore value, as some Amish quiltmakers did, but it's helpful to understand it. When fabrics of contrasting value are placed side by side, patchwork intersections become more pronounced and a design emerges along the contrasting edge. Keep in mind that the perceived value of a fabric depends on the fabric against which it is positioned. For example, medium blue looks dark when positioned against a pastel, but it looks light to medium when positioned against black.

Begin sorting fabrics by value. Place fabrics that are similar in value side by side by pinning them to a design wall or bulletin board. Step back and view the entire group. The fabrics should all blend together. If any fabric appears noticeably lighter or darker than others in the group, remove it. Add and subtract fabrics until you have a good assortment for that particular value. Repeat the process for remaining value groups. A value filter might help you make value determinations. These inexpensive red plastic filters mask color, making objects appear as shades of gray or black—the way color appears in a black and white photograph, for example.

One element often found in Amish quilts is referred to as "sparkle." When an occasional pale, clear fabric is positioned next to a very dark fabric, it creates an almost twinkling impression, especially under soft lighting like that found in an

Amish home. Avoid using too much sparkle, or the effect will be minimized.

Color Wheels

It might be helpful to consider a color wheel when making fabric selections. The three primary colors, red, yellow, and blue, are shown in **Diagram 1A.** If equal amounts of two primary colors are mixed, the results are midway between the two colors, or purple, orange, and green, as shown in **1B.** If the mixture is unequal, the resulting color is more closely related to the original primary. For example, if red and blue are mixed, but the mixture contains more red than blue, the result is magenta, rather than purple or violet, as shown in **1C.**

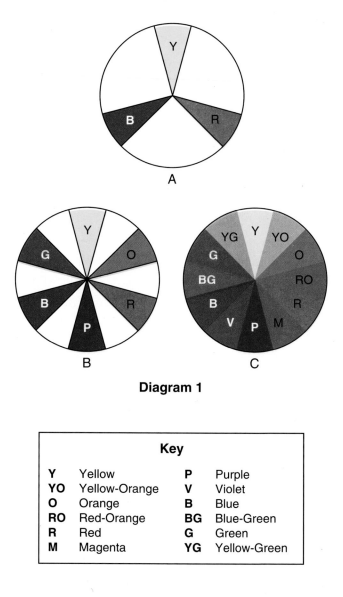

Diagram 1

Key			
Y	Yellow	**P**	Purple
YO	Yellow-Orange	**V**	Violet
O	Orange	**B**	Blue
RO	Red-Orange	**BG**	Blue-Green
R	Red	**G**	Green
M	Magenta	**YG**	Yellow-Green

There are four basic ways to approach a color scheme, as shown in **Diagram 2**. For a monochromatic look, select one color on the color wheel and use only shades of that color. Value is critical and must be varied for the design to emerge. For an analogous color scheme, select any three adjacent colors on the color wheel. To use complementary colors, select two colors opposite each other on the color wheel. For a triadic color scheme, choose three colors that are spaced evenly around the color wheel, like purple, orange, and green.

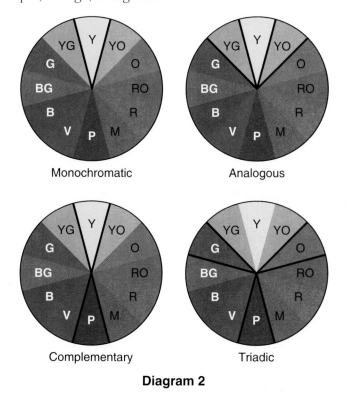

Monochromatic   Analogous

Complementary   Triadic

Diagram 2

Try creating the different color schemes with swatches of fabric to see if one is more appealing to you than another. Remember, these schemes are only a starting point; the variations of each color within a given family are endless. Be sure to consider all tones and shadings of a particular color for your quilt.

MAKING TRIANGLE SQUARES

Many Amish quilts, including a handful featured in this book, feature triangle squares. A triangle square is made of two right triangles sewn together along their longest sides to make a square, as shown in **Diagram 3**. Both of the techniques described here will help you assemble accurate triangle squares more quickly than you could using the traditional method of sewing individual triangles together. Examples for both methods produce finished triangle squares that are 2¾ inches, as used in the Broken Dishes quilt on page 36. If you need triangle squares in a different size, follow the directions below.

Diagram 3

Method 1: Grids

The grid method is a good choice if you plan to make many identical triangle squares. Two pieces of fabric are cut oversize, placed together with right sides facing, then marked, sewn, and cut apart into individual triangle squares. This technique requires careful marking and sewing, but it produces multiples of identical triangle squares quickly and allows you to avoid working with bias edges. It is an especially useful method when working with very small triangle squares because your results may be more accurate than with other piecing methods.

To make a Broken Dishes quilt similar to the one on page 36, variety is important and can be achieved by using grids with fewer squares. Adjust the number of squares in the grid to suit the design you are trying to achieve.

Step 1. To determine the correct size to cut the fabric, you must first determine the number of triangle squares you wish to make and the dimensions of the squares in the grid. Each square drawn in the grid will result in two triangle squares and is equal to the finished size of the triangle square, plus ⅞ inch.

In this example, the finished size of the triangle

square is 2¾ inches. The number of identical triangle squares required is 60, so:

60 triangle squares required ÷ 2 completed triangle squares in each grid square = a grid of 30 squares

Grid size = finished size of 2¾ inches + ⅞ inch = 3⅝-inch grid required

A grid of 5 squares by 6 squares produces 60 triangle squares and measures 18⅛ × 21¾ inches. To allow a bit of extra fabric on all sides, choose two pieces of fabric that are at least 19½ × 22¾ inches.

Note: If your fabric cuts are narrow, adjust the grid layout. For instance, a grid of three squares by ten squares will yield the same number of triangle squares but can be drawn on a piece of fabric that measures approximately 11½ × 37 inches.

Step 2. On the wrong side of the lighter fabric, use a pencil or permanent marker to draw a grid of squares, as shown in **Diagram 4A**. Begin approximately ½ inch from the edge of the fabric. Referring to **4B**, carefully draw a diagonal line through each square in the grid; these lines will be cutting lines.

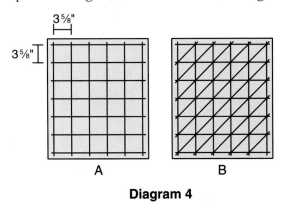

Diagram 4

Step 3. Position the marked fabric and the second piece of fabric with their right sides together. Press to help the two pieces adhere to each other and use a few straight pins to secure the layers. Using a ¼-inch seam allowance, stitch along both sides of the diagonal lines, as shown in **Diagram 5**. Use the edge of your presser foot as a ¼-inch guide, or draw a line ¼ inch from each side of the diagonal line to indicate sewing lines.

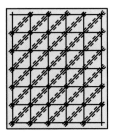

Diagram 5

Step 4. Use a rotary cutter and ruler to cut the grid apart. Cut on all the grid and diagonal lines, as shown in **Diagram 6A**. Carefully press the triangle squares open, pressing each seam toward the darker fabric. Trim off the triangle points at the seam ends, as shown in **6B**. Continue marking and cutting triangle squares until you have made the number required for the quilt you are making.

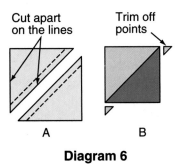

Cut apart on the lines   Trim off points

A   B

Diagram 6

Method 2: Single Squares

If you prefer a scrappier look or if you would like to make use of small pieces of fabric, the individual square method may be useful. Squares of different fabrics are sandwiched and sewn together, then cut apart diagonally to yield two identical triangle squares.

Step 1. Determine the required size of fabric squares by adding ⅞ inch to the desired finished size of your triangle squares. For a 2¾-inch triangle square, you must cut 3⅝-inch squares of fabric.

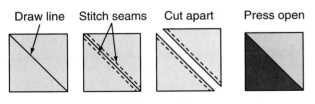

— Sew Easy —

To make the finished size of your squares as accurate as possible, cut fabric squares slightly larger than necessary, then trim back the completed triangle squares after assembly.

Step 2. Select two fabrics for a triangle square and cut a 3⅝-inch square from each. Draw a diagonal line from one corner to the other on the wrong side of the lightest square. Position the squares with their right sides together, taking care to align all edges. Sew a seam ¼ inch from each side of the drawn line. After sewing the seams, cut the squares in half on the drawn line. Press the seam in each triangle square toward the darkest fabric (see **Diagram 7**).

Draw line   Stitch seams   Cut apart   Press open

Diagram 7

Step 3. Continue making triangle squares until you have completed the total number required for your quilt. If you are sewing many triangle squares, chain piecing will help speed up the process. Draw diagonal lines and pair each square with its counterpart. Feed the units through the sewing machine one after another in a continuous chain, without breaking the threads.

QUILTING

One of the most recognized aspects of Amish quiltmaking is intricate hand quilting. Very small running stitches are the hallmark of an experienced Amish quilter. Even though quilting stitches add depth and beauty to a quilt, the Amish view hand quilting as purely functional—it serves to hold the layers of the quilt securely together. While the world around her may have little influence on an Amish woman's daily activities in most instances, hand-quilting designs are often seen as an exception. Borrowing from everyday life, the Amish have incorporated recognizable objects into their quilting. Feather, cable, basket, star, and pumpkin seed quilting designs can be seen in many antique Amish quilts and are incorporated into many Amish-style quilts created today.

The traditional Amish quilting patterns shown below and on pages 110–111 can be enlarged or reduced to suit your needs. Feathered circles and swirls, cables, and pumpkin seeds are often used on borders, while baskets, stars, and cross-hatching are quilted into setting squares and triangles. Use your imagination to combine or adapt these patterns.

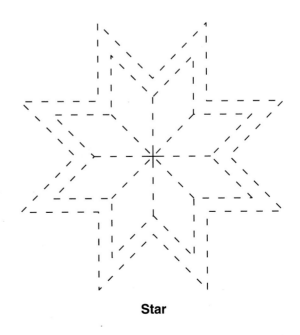

Star

Enlarge or reduce on a photocopier to fit your quilt.

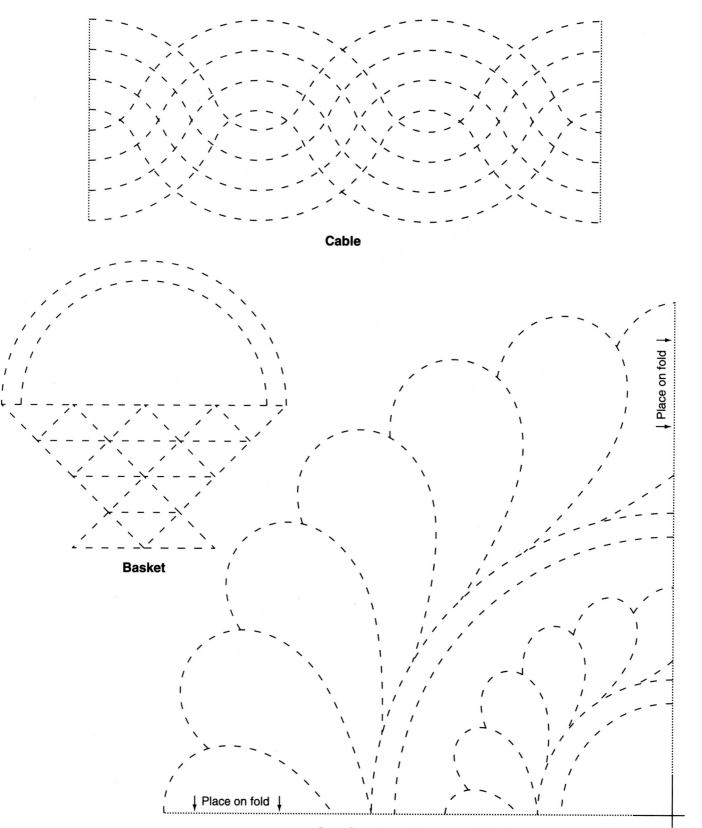

Cable

Basket

↓ Place on fold ↓

Place on fold →

One-Quarter of Feathered Circle

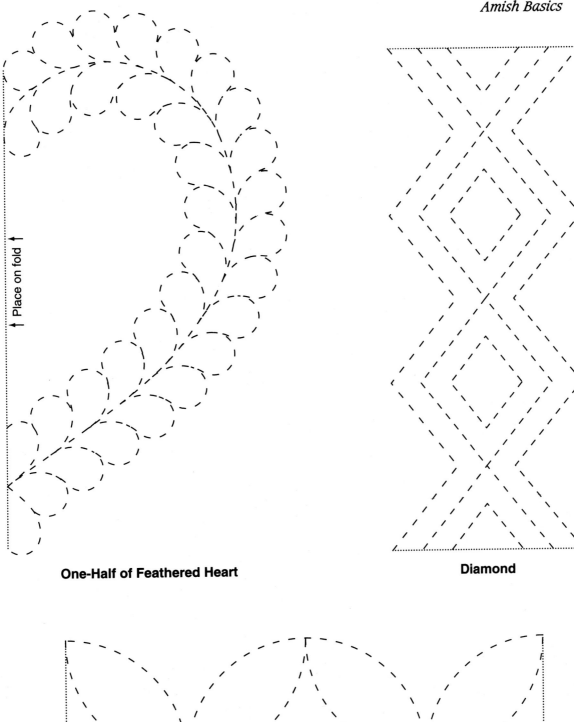

↑ Place on fold ↑

One-Half of Feathered Heart

Diamond

Pumpkin Seed

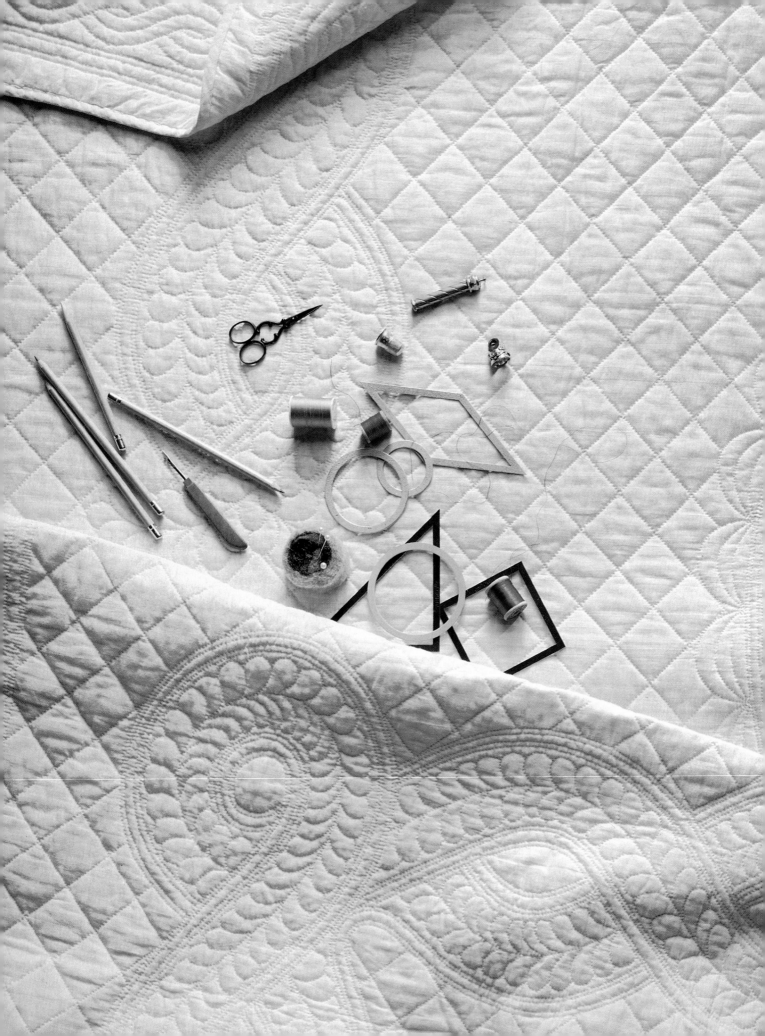

QUILTMAKING
BASICS

This section provides a refresher course in basic quiltmaking techniques. Refer to it as needed; it will help not only with the projects in this book but also with all your quiltmaking.

QUILTMAKER'S BASIC SUPPLY LIST

Here's a list of items you should have on hand before beginning a project.

• **Iron and ironing board:** Make sure these are set up near your sewing machine. Careful pressing leads to accurate piecing.

• **Needles:** The two types of needles commonly used by quilters are *betweens*, short needles used for hand quilting, and *sharps*, long, very thin needles used for appliqué and hand piecing. The thickness of hand-sewing needles decreases as their size designation increases. For instance, a size 12 needle is smaller than a size 10.

• **Rotary cutter, plastic ruler, and cutting mat:** Fabric can be cut quickly and accurately with rotary-cutting equipment. There are a variety of cutters available, all with slightly different handle styles and safety latches. Rigid, see-through acrylic rulers are used with rotary cutters. A 6 × 24-inch ruler is a good size; for the most versatility, be sure it has 45 and 60 degree angle markings. A 14-inch square ruler will also be helpful for making sure blocks are square. Always use a special mat with a rotary cutter. The mat protects the work surface and helps to grip the fabric. Purchase the largest mat practical for your sewing area. A good all-purpose size is 18 × 24 inches.

• **Safety pins:** These are generally used to baste quilts for machine quilting. Use rustproof nickel-plated brass safety pins, preferably in size #0.

• **Scissors:** You'll need several pairs of scissors—shears for cutting fabric, general scissors for cutting paper and template plastic, and small, sharp embroidery scissors for trimming threads.

• **Seam ripper:** A seam ripper with a small, extra-fine blade slips easily under any stitch length.

• **Sewing machine:** Any machine with a straight stitch is suitable for piecing quilt blocks. Follow the manufacturer's recommendations for cleaning and servicing your sewing machine.

• **Straight pins:** Choose long, thin pins with glass or plastic heads that are easy to see against fabric so that you don't forget to remove one.

• **Template material:** Sheets of clear and opaque template plastic can be purchased at most quilt or craft shops. Gridded plastic is also available and may help you to draw shapes more easily. Various weights of cardboard can also be used for templates, including common household items like cereal boxes, poster board, and manila file folders.

• **Thimbles:** For hand quilting, a thimble is almost essential. Look for one that fits the finger you use to push the needle. The thimble should be snug enough to stay put when you shake your hand. There should be a bit of space between the end of your finger and the inside of the thimble.

• **Thread:** For hand or machine piecing, 100 percent cotton thread is a traditional favorite. Cotton-covered polyester is also acceptable. For hand quilting, use 100 percent cotton quilting thread. For machine quilting, you may want to try clear nylon thread as the top thread, with cotton thread in the bobbin.

• **Tweezers:** Keep a pair of tweezers handy for removing bits of thread from ripped-out seams and for pulling away scraps of removable foundations. Regular cosmetic tweezers will work fine.

SELECTING AND PREPARING FABRICS

The traditional fabric choice for quilts is 100 percent cotton. It handles well, is easy to care for, presses easily, and frays less than synthetic blends.

The yardages in this book are generous estimates based on 44/45-inch-wide fabrics. It's a good idea to always purchase a bit more fabric than necessary to compensate for shrinkage and occasional cutting errors.

Prewash your fabrics using warm water and a mild soap or detergent. Test for colorfastness by first soaking a scrap in warm water. If colors bleed, set the dye by soaking the whole piece of fabric in a solution of 3 parts cold water to 1 part vinegar. Rinse the fabric several times in warm water. If it still bleeds, don't use it in a quilt that will need laundering—save it for a wallhanging that won't get a lot of use.

After washing, preshrink your fabric by drying it in a dryer on the medium setting. To keep wrinkles under control, remove the fabric from the dryer while it's still slightly damp and press it immediately with a hot iron.

CUTTING FABRIC

The cutting instructions for each project follow the list of materials. Whenever possible, the instructions are written to take advantage of quick rotary-cutting techniques. In addition, some projects include patterns for those who prefer to make templates and scissor cut individual pieces.

Although rotary cutting can be faster and more accurate than cutting with scissors, it has one disadvantage: It does not always result in the most efficient use of fabric. In some cases, the method results in long strips of leftover fabric. Don't think of these as waste; just add them to your scrap bag for future projects.

Rotary-Cutting Basics

Follow these two safety rules every time you use a rotary cutter: Always cut *away* from yourself, and always slide the blade guard into place as soon as you stop cutting.

Step 1: You can cut several layers of fabric at a time with a rotary cutter. Fold the fabric with the selvage edges together. You can fold it again if you want, doubling the number of layers to be cut.

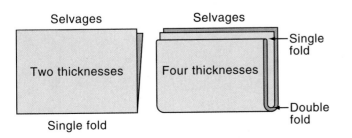

Step 2: To square up the end of the fabric, place a ruled square on the fold and slide a 6 × 24-inch ruler against the side of the square. Hold the ruler in place, remove the square, and cut along the edge of the ruler. If you are left-handed, work from the other end of the fabric.

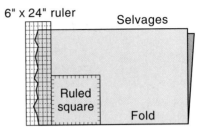

Step 3: For patchwork, cut strips or rectangles on the crosswise grain, then subcut them into smaller pieces as needed. The diagram shows a strip cut into squares.

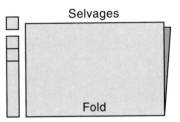

Step 4: A square can be subcut into two triangles by making one diagonal cut (A). Two diagonal cuts yield four triangles (B).

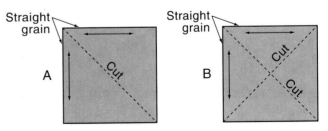

Step 5: Check strips periodically to make sure they're straight and not angled. If they are angled, refold the fabric and square up the edges again.

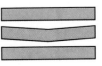

ENLARGING PATTERNS

Every effort has been made to provide full-size pattern pieces. But in some cases, where the pattern piece is too large to fit on the page, only one-half or one-quarter of the pattern is given. Instructions on the pattern piece will tell you where to position the pattern to continue tracing to make a full-size template.

MAKING AND USING TEMPLATES

To make a plastic template, place template plastic over the book page, trace the pattern onto the plastic, and cut out the template. To make a cardboard template, copy the pattern onto tracing paper, glue the paper to the cardboard, and cut out the template. With a permanent marker, record on every template any identification letters and grain lines, as well as the size and name of the block and the number of pieces needed. Always check your templates against the printed pattern for accuracy.

The patchwork patterns in this book are printed with double lines. The inner dashed line is the finished size of the piece, while the outer solid line includes seam allowance.

For hand piecing: Trace the inner line to make finished-size templates. Cut out the templates on the traced line. Draw around the templates on the wrong side of the fabric, leaving ½ inch between pieces. Then mark ¼-inch seam allowances before you cut out the pieces.

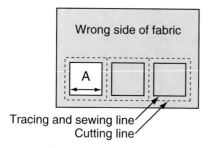

Wrong side of fabric

A

Tracing and sewing line
Cutting line

For machine piecing: Trace the outer solid line on the printed pattern to make templates with seam allowance included. Draw around the templates on the wrong side of the fabric and cut out the pieces on this line.

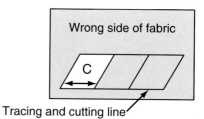

Wrong side of fabric

C

Tracing and cutting line

For appliqué: Appliqué patterns in this book have only a single line and are finished size. Draw around the templates on the right side of the fabric, leaving ½ inch between pieces. Add ⅛- to ¼-inch seam allowances by eye as you cut the pieces.

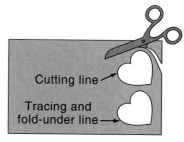

Cutting line

Tracing and
fold-under line

PIECING BASICS

Standard seam allowance for piecing is ¼ inch. Machine sew a sample seam to test the accuracy of the seam allowance; adjust as needed. For hand piecing, the sewing line is marked on the fabric.

Hand Piecing

Cut fabric pieces using finished-size templates. Place the pieces right sides together, match marked seam lines, and pin. Use a running stitch along the marked line, backstitching every four or five stitches and at the beginning and end of the seam.

When you cross seam allowances of previously joined units, leave the seam allowances free. Backstitch just before you cross, slip the needle through the seam allowance, backstitch just after you cross, then resume stitching the seam.

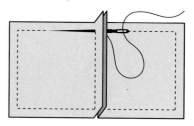

Machine Piecing

Cut the fabric pieces using templates with seam allowances included or using a rotary cutter and ruler without templates. Set the stitch length at 10 to 12 stitches per inch.

Place the fabric pieces right sides together, then sew from raw edge to raw edge. Press seams before crossing them with other seams, pressing toward the darker fabric whenever possible.

Chain piecing: Use this technique when you need to sew more than one of the same type of unit. Place the fabric pieces right sides together and, without lifting the presser foot or cutting the thread, run the pairs through the sewing machine one after another. Once all the units you need have been sewn, snip them apart and press.

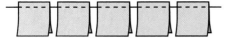

Setting In Pieces

Pattern pieces must sometimes be set into angles created by other pieces, as shown in the diagram. Here, pieces A, B, and C are set into the angles created by the four joined diamond pieces.

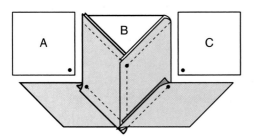

Step 1: Keep the seam allowances open where the piece is to be set in. Begin by sewing the first seam in the usual manner, beginning and ending the seam ¼ inch from the edge of the fabric and backstitching at each end.

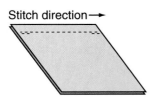

Stitch direction →

Step 2: Open up the pattern pieces and place the piece to be set in right sides together with one of the first two pieces. Begin the seam ¼ inch from the edge of the fabric and sew to the exact point where the first seam ended, backstitching at the beginning and end of the seam.

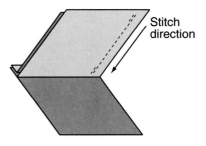

Stitch direction

Step 3: Rotate the pattern pieces so that you are ready to sew the final seam. Keeping the seam allowances free, sew from the point where the last seam ended to ¼ inch from the edge of the piece.

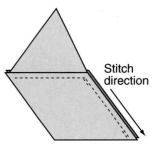

Stitch direction

Step 4: Press the seams so that as many of them as possible lie flat. The finished unit should look like the one shown here.

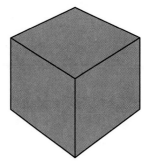

APPLIQUÉ BASICS

Review "Making and Using Templates" to learn how to prepare templates for appliqué. Lightly draw around each template on the right side of the fabric using a pencil or other nonpermanent marker. These are the fold-under lines. Cut out the pieces ⅛ to ¼ inch to the outside of the marked lines.

The Needle-Turn Method

Pin the pieces in position on the background fabric, always working in order from the background to the foreground. For best results, don't turn under or appliqué edges that will be covered by other appliqué pieces. Use a thread color that matches the fabric of the appliqué piece.

Step 1: Bring the needle up from under the appliqué patch exactly on the drawn line. Fold under the seam allowance on the line to neatly encase the knot.

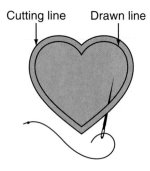

Cutting line   Drawn line

Step 2: Insert the tip of the needle into the background fabric right next to where the thread comes out of the appliqué piece. Bring the needle out of the background fabric approximately ¹⁄₁₆ inch away from and up through the very edge of the fold, completing the first stitch.

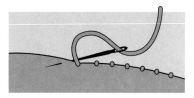

Step 3: Repeat this process for each stitch, using the tip and shank of your appliqué needle to turn under ½-inch-long sections of seam allowance at a time. As you turn under a section, press it flat with your thumb and then stitch it in place, as shown.

Pressing Basics

Proper pressing can make a big difference in the appearance of a finished block or quilt top. It allows patchwork to open up to its full size, permits more precise matching of seams, and results in smooth, flat work. Quilters are divided on the issue of whether a steam or dry iron is best; experiment to see which works best for you. Keep these tips in mind:

• Press seam allowances to one side, not open. Whenever possible, press toward the darker fabric. If you find you must press toward a lighter fabric, trim the dark seam allowance slightly to prevent show-through.

• Press seams of adjacent rows of blocks, or rows within blocks, in opposite directions. The pressed seams will fit together snugly, producing precise intersections.

• Press, don't iron. Bring the iron down gently and firmly. This is especially important if you are using steam.

• To press appliqués, lay a towel on the ironing board, turn the piece right side down on the towel, and press very gently on the back side.

Assembling Quilt Tops

Lay out all the blocks for your quilt top using the quilt diagram or photo as a guide to placement. Pin and sew the blocks together in vertical or horizontal rows for straight-set quilts and in diagonal rows for diagonal-set quilts. Press the seam allowances in opposite directions from row to row so that the seams will fit together snugly when rows are joined.

To keep a large quilt top manageable, join rows into pairs first and then join the pairs. When pressing a completed quilt top, press on the back side first, carefully clipping and removing hanging threads; then press the front.

MITERING BORDERS

Step 1: Start by measuring the length of your finished quilt top through the center. Add to that figure two times the width of the border, plus 5 inches extra. This is the length you need to cut the two side borders. For example, if the quilt top is 48 inches long and the border is 4 inches wide, you need two borders that are each 61 inches long (48 + 4 + 4 + 5 = 61). In the same manner, calculate the length of the top and bottom borders, then cut the borders.

Step 2: Sew each of the borders to the quilt top, beginning and ending the seams ¼ inch from the edge of the quilt. Press the border seams flat from the right side of the quilt.

Step 3: Working at one corner of the quilt, place one border on top of the adjacent border. Fold the top border under so that it meets the edge of the other border and forms a 45 degree angle, as shown in the diagram. If you are working with a plaid or striped border, check to make sure the stripes match along this folded edge. Press the fold in place.

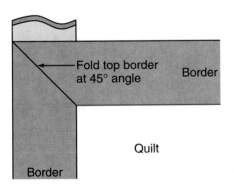

Step 4: Fold the quilt top with right sides together and align the edges of the borders. With the pressed fold as the corner seam line and the

body of the quilt out of the way, sew from the inner corner to the outer corner, as shown in the diagram.

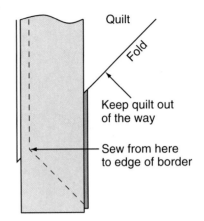

Step 5: Unfold the quilt and check to make sure that all points match and the miter is flat. Trim the border seam allowance to ¼ inch and press the seam open.

Step 6: Repeat Steps 3 through 5 for the three remaining borders.

MARKING QUILTING DESIGNS

To mark a quilting design, use a commercially made stencil, make your own stencil using a sheet of plastic, or trace the design from a book page. Use a nonpermanent marker, such as a silver or white pencil, chalk pencil, or chalk marker, that will be visible on the fabric. You can even mark with a 0.5 mm lead pencil, but be sure to mark lightly.

If you are using a quilt design from this book, either trace the design onto tracing paper or photocopy it. If the pattern will be used many times, glue it to cardboard to make it sturdy.

For light-color fabrics that you can see through, place the pattern under the quilt top and trace the quilting design directly onto the fabric. Mark in a thin, continuous line that will be covered by the quilting thread.

With dark fabrics, mark from the top by drawing around a hard-edged design template. To make a simple template, trace the design onto template plastic and cut it out around the outer edge. Trace around the template onto the fabric, then add inner lines by eye.

LAYERING AND BASTING

Carefully preparing the quilt top, batting, and backing will ensure that the finished quilt will lie flat and smooth. Place the backing wrong side up on a large table or clean floor. Center the batting on the backing and smooth out any wrinkles. Center the quilt top right side up on the batting; smooth it out and remove any loose threads.

If you plan to hand quilt, baste the quilt with thread. Use a long darning needle and white thread. Baste outward from the center of the quilt in a grid of horizontal and vertical rows approximately 4 inches apart.

If you plan to machine quilt, baste with safety pins. Thread basting does not hold the layers securely enough during machine quilting, plus the thread is more difficult to remove when quilting is completed. Use rustproof nickel-plated brass safety pins in size #0, starting in the center of the quilt and pinning approximately every 3 inches.

HAND QUILTING

For best results, use a hoop or a frame to hold the quilt layers taut and smooth during quilting. Work with one hand on top of the quilt and the other hand underneath, guiding the needle. Don't worry about the size of your stitches in the beginning; concentrate on making them even, and they will get smaller over time.

Getting started: Thread a needle with quilting thread and knot the end. Insert the needle through the quilt top and batting about 1 inch away from where you will begin stitching. Bring the needle to the surface in position to make the first stitch. Gently tug on the thread to pop the knot through the quilt top and bury it in the batting.

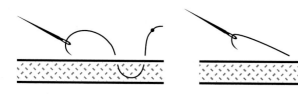

Taking the stitches: Insert the needle through the three layers of the quilt. When you feel the tip of the needle with your underneath finger, gently guide it back up through the quilt. When the needle comes through the top of the quilt, press your thimble on the end with the eye to guide it down again through the quilt layers. Continue to quilt in this manner, taking two or three small running stitches at a time.

Ending a line of stitching: Bring the needle to the top of the quilt just past the last stitch. Make a knot at the surface by bringing the needle under the thread where it comes out of the fabric and up through the loop of thread it creates. Repeat this knot and insert the needle into the hole where the thread comes out of the fabric. Run the needle inside the batting for an inch and bring it back to the surface. Tug gently on the thread to pop the knot into the batting layer. Clip the thread.

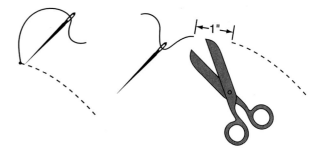

MACHINE QUILTING

For best results when doing machine-guided quilting, use a walking foot (also called an even feed foot) on your sewing machine. For free-motion quilting, use a darning or machine-embroidery foot.

Use thread to match the fabric colors, or use clear nylon thread in the top of the machine and a white or colored thread in the bobbin. To secure the thread at the beginning of a line of stitches, adjust the stitch length on your machine to make several very short stitches, then gradually increase to the regular stitch length. As you near the end of the line, gradually reduce the stitch length so that the last few stitches are very short.

For machine-guided quilting, keep the feed dogs up and move all three layers as smoothly as you can under the needle. To turn a corner in a quilting design, stop with the needle inserted in the fabric, raise the foot, pivot the quilt, lower the foot, and continue stitching.

For free-motion quilting, disengage the feed dogs so you can manipulate the quilt freely as you stitch. Guide the quilt under the needle with both hands, coordinating the speed of the needle with the movement of the quilt to create stitches of consistent length.

MAKING AND ATTACHING BINDING

Double-fold binding, which is also called French-fold binding, can be made from either straight-grain or bias strips. To make double-fold binding, cut strips of fabric four times the finished width of the binding, plus seam allowance. In general, cut strips 2 inches wide for quilts with thin batting or scalloped edges and $2\frac{1}{4}$ to $2\frac{1}{2}$ inches wide for quilts with thicker batting.

Straight-Grain Binding

To make straight-grain binding, cut crosswise strips from the binding fabric in the desired width. Sew them together end to end with diagonal seams.

Place the strips with right sides together so that each strip is set in $\frac{1}{4}$ inch from the end of the other strip. Sew a diagonal seam and trim the excess fabric, leaving a $\frac{1}{4}$-inch seam allowance.

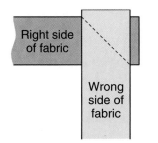

Continuous Bias Binding

Bias binding can be cut in one long strip from a square of fabric that has been cut apart and resewn into a tube. To estimate the number of inches of binding a particular square will produce, use this formula:

Multiply the length of one side by the length of another side, and divide the result by the width of binding you want. Using a 30-inch square and $2\frac{1}{4}$-inch binding as an example: $30 \times 30 = 900$; $900 \div 2\frac{1}{4} = 400$ inches of binding.

Step 1: To make bias binding, cut a square in half diagonally to get two triangles. Place the two triangles right sides together, as shown, and sew with a $\frac{1}{4}$-inch seam. Open out the two pieces and press the seam open.

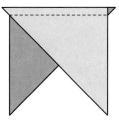

Step 2: Using a pencil and a see-through ruler, mark cutting lines on the wrong side of the fabric in the desired binding width. Draw the lines parallel to the bias edges.

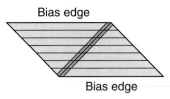

Step 3: Fold the fabric with right sides together, bringing the two nonbias edges together and offsetting them by one strip width (as shown in the diagram at the top of page 122). Pin the edges together, creating a tube, and sew with a $\frac{1}{4}$-inch seam. Press the seam open.

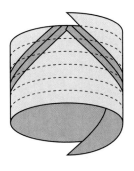

Step 4: Cut on the marked lines, turning the tube to cut one long bias strip.

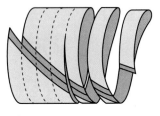

Attaching the Binding

Trim excess batting and backing even with the quilt top. For double-fold binding, fold the long binding strip in half lengthwise, with wrong sides together, and press. Beginning in the middle of a side, not in a corner, place the strip right sides together with the quilt top, align raw edges, and pin.

Step 1: Fold over approximately 1 inch at the beginning of the strip and begin stitching ½ inch from the fold. Sew the binding to the quilt, using a ¼-inch seam and stitching through all layers.

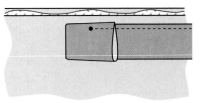

Step 2: As you approach a corner, stop stitching ¼ inch from the raw edge of the corner. Backstitch and remove the quilt from the machine. Fold the binding strip up at a 45 degree angle, as shown in the following diagram on the left. Fold the strip back down so there is a fold at the upper

edge, as shown on the right. Begin sewing ¼ inch from the top edge of the quilt, continuing to the next corner. Miter all four corners in this manner.

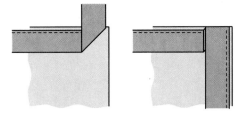

Step 3: To finish the binding seam, overlap the folded-back beginning section with the ending section. Stitch across the fold, allowing the end to extend approximately ½ inch beyond the beginning.

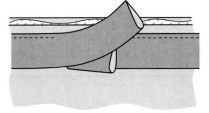

Step 4: Turn the binding to the back of the quilt and blindstitch the folded edge in place, covering the machine stitches with the folded edge. Fold in the adjacent sides on the back and take several stitches in the miter. In the same way, add several stitches to the miters on the front.

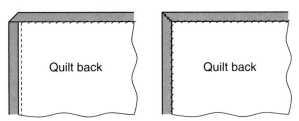

SIGNING YOUR QUILT

Be sure to sign and date your finished quilt. Your finishing touch can be a simple signature in permanent ink or an elaborate inked or embroidered label. Add any other pertinent details that can help family members or quilt collectors 100 years from now understand what went into your labor of love.